PROPHET IS...

The School of the Apostles & Prophets - - -

LETHAL WEAPON

#1 *"Since I have been Called to Preach, Now What???"*

    Understand the calling is not the Commission to Go, be trained, be developed, be mentored come into the ....

. . . . PROPHETIC FLOW!

THE 5-FOLD OFFICES OF GOVERNMENTS

A manual for the believer who desires to go beyond the VEIL of tradition. . . . .

What is the school of the Prophets/Apostle? It is a training school for those called to the prophetic ministry as well as for individuals who desire a better understanding of the prophetic ministry. These are the days wherein God is moving by His Spirit and is taking the offices of the Apostle and the prophet out of the closet and out from hiding. He is thereby opening the eyes of the body of Christ that she might behold what has been in the midst of her all the time! It is a common misunderstanding to think that apostles and prophets ceased to exist after the death of the 12 disciples or to believe that they're not present in the body of Christ today. There have been many ministers thought to be evangelists and pastors who are God appointed and anointed prophets, but because of prejudices and misunderstandings, they have been unable to stand in the office God has called them. We invite you to come and explore the Scriptures with us, to discover what the Word of God actually says about the office and calling of God's prophets. Perhaps you feel that you have been called to be an oracle of the Lord and have difficulty explaining your experiences of finding someone that you could relate to and learn from. The School of the Prophets/Apostles is for you!

Prophet Israel

iUniverse books may be ordered through booksellers or by contacting:

iUniverse
1663 Liberty Drive
Bloomington, IN 47403
www.iuniverse.com
1-800-Authors (1-800-288-4677)

Because of the dynamic nature of the Internet, any Web addresses or links contained in this book may have changed since publication and may no longer be valid. The views expressed in this work are solely those of the author and do not necessarily reflect the views of the publisher, and the publisher hereby disclaims any responsibility for them.

ISBN: 978-1-4401-6383-8 (sc)
ISBN: 978-1-4401-6384-5 (ebook)

Printed in the United States of America

iUniverse rev. date: 05/19/2010

TABLE OF CONTENTS

INTRODUCTION

Hosea 4:6 "My people are destroyed (paralyzed without truth) for the lack of knowledge".

Apostle Paul speaks to us to "grow in grace and in the knowledge of our Lord and Saviour Jesus Christ." Knowledge in the Greek means "gnosis" full knowledge, knowledge received through in-depth relationship or intercourse.

When wisdom is not at the mouth of the Priest's lips, then the spirit of religious tradition which releases the spirit of error is received and believers walk and grope in the darkness.

This manual is a training tool for further study and investigation in the Ministry of the Apostle and Prophet. Allowing the believer to understand the role of the Apostle and the Prophet in the end time. We need a prophet in every city, state and nation.

May your eyes be opened, may supernatural power come upon you, may you be impregnated with prophetic and apostolic revelation. May the prophetic anointing come off each page causing you to come into the "Prophetic Flow"!

Dedication

To all the believers who are assigned to the Apostolic, Prophetic Movement, Apostle Roper, whom I love dearly for mentoring and seeing me through seasons of uncertainty,

You are an apostolic seed!

A charge to keep I have
A God to glorify
Every dying soul be saved
Fitted for the sky

To serve this present age
A calling to fulfill
All my strength engaged
To do the Masters will!!

There is a clear Third Millennium apostolic and prophetic mandate for the church. The Gospel of the Kingdom of God must be preached not only to individuals, but to systems, institutions, and nations; Only then will Biblical reform take place. We have yet to enter into the greatest era of the Church's global and encompassing impact. A militant church, preaching and applying Biblical law to politics, government, economics, education, technology, entertainment, law, media, biotechnology, foreign policy, business, etc., is the Third Millennium model. In the *Prophetic Anointing for the 21st Century*, my friend Prophet Israel has written a timely apostolic and prophetic caveat. May we discern its revelation, heed its message, and apply its principles.

Prophet James L. Giles
Dominion Christian Embassy
Charlotte, North Carolina

Eagle Spirits Introduction

The picture that caused you to purchase this manual is a prophetic statement of who you are, designed as an Eagle Saint by the Father before the foundation of the world.

The eagle is a bird that flies alone. Eagles fly in realms and atmospheres that other birds only dream of. You are an Eagle Saint, eagles are rare birds, their appetite is unlike most other birds. They eat fresh revelation. Their diet is very expensive. You will never see an eagle in a congregation of chicken hawks. Eagles fly with other eagles. Eagles don't allow other birds to determine the activity or the circumference of their rule and the jurisdiction of their dominion in the earth. Eagles change their nests each year. Eagles travel on eagles airlines. Eagles drive eagles cars. Eagles go from glory to glory to glory. That's why many have mistaken your purpose, that's why many have rejected you from their small nests. Eagles have expanded mentalities. Eagles cannot survive on the food that buzzards eat, you are an Eagle Saint, your depths in Christ, your wings span, your height in revelation, your acronomical abilities frighten common birds, conquer your fears, remove your doubts, let go of your past, come into the new, and have divine wisdom, you have divine light, you have divine intelligence in you! You are destined for greatness, you are destined to be rich, and you are God's original design!! Fly high. You live in the high places, you live in the secret places of the most high, fly high... You will no longer be confused about who you are, there is no comparison of your creativity, your brilliance, your radiance, your beauty, your vision, no comparison of your love, you know your origin and what species you were destined to fly with, you are an Eagle Saint, you are God's original design, you were uniquely made in the Maker's image. No two fingerprints are the same, you are an offspring of Jehovah, open your wings and fly, but remember you will intimidate most common birds, don't condescend to their level, don't be concerned about their negative attitude in regards to the altitudes you fly in. Find other eagles and soar with them, destiny means connection, God never designed Adam to be alone, He sent Eve an Eagle Saint to take him to the next level. Seek the eagles out, they live in royalty, prosperity, and elegance and eat the riches of the kingdom, don't get distracted at what other species are doing, waiting to go to heaven, when you are bringing the demonstration of the manifestation of true sons and daughters of divinity in the earth, oh the glory you carry. They are waiting on the coming revival, you represent the reformation!! You don't fit in their boxes or circles, you are in a class all by yourself, you are a part of a new breed of prophetic leadership, there is no pattern to follow, you are the pattern... Come fly into the prophetic realms..... mend your broken wings and broken dreams, you were ordained to fly high, you were ordained as God's original design. A masterpiece in the making.....

Proverbs 30:19 The way of the eagle is in the air,

Deut 32:11 As an eagle stirreth up her nest, fluttereth over her young, spreadeth abroad her wing, taketh them, beareth them on her eagles wings, so the Lord alone did lead him, and there was no strange god with Him, He made him to ride on the high places of the earth.

Ex: 19:4 And how I bare you on eagles wings and brought you unto myself.

Ps 103:5 Who satisfieth thy mouth with good things so that thy youth is renewed like an eagle.

Isaiah 40:31 But they that wait upon the Lord shall renew their strength, they shall mount up with wings as eagles, they shall run and not be weary, they shall walk and never faint. Prophet Barsh

COME INTO THE PROPHETIC FLOW

THE SCHOOL OF THE PROPHETS & APOSTLES

1. Elisha called Elijah his_____. II Kings 2:12
2. If you are called to minister, you are called to_____.
3. In the Old Testament there were 5 places of training:
   R_____, G_____,
   B_____
   J_____, and J_____
4. Elijah started the School of the
   _____.
5. S_____ started the _____of
   the_____.
6. As there appointed leader Samuel brought O_____,
   D_____
   S_____, and C_____.
7. You don't call yourself a P_____ because you prophesy.
8. Bethel means H_____.
9. One of the signs of a true prophet is that you will see
   M_____.
10. The measure of your s_____ to authority determines the
    degree of a _____, which you should move in.
11. Never place a man in authority with character
    d_____.
12. Jeremiah 1:5 said... Before I f_____thee in the belly, I knew
    thee, before thou comest forth out of the w_____ I
    o_____thee a P_____ unto the
    nations.
13. A Prophet is an ordained c_____.
14. Name the five (5) Fold Ministry Gifts.
    1._____ 2._____
    3._____
    4._____ 5._____
15. You only prophesy to the level of r_____.
16. The 3 (three) primary reasons for prophecy is for
    E_____,
    E_____ and
    E_____.
17. After salvation then one must be filled with the H_____
    G_____,
    and trained to be placed in the ministry of H_____ and
    G_____.
18. All ministries must flow out of divine
    r_____.
19. Everyone in the house of God must be under a _____.

6.

20. Name the 4 realms of prophetic gifts. I Cor. 12:6 M_____ of prophecy. Rom. 12:4

    G_____ gift of prophecy. Rev. 19:10 the

    S_____ of prophecy and Ephesians 4:11

    O_____ of the P_____.

21. Music in the Prophetic ministry demands that the Minstrel, Psalmist and the Prophet be married to the House of God.

22. Female prophets were D_____ (Judges 4:4)

    M_____ (Exodus 15:20),

    H_____ (IKing 22:14) and Isaiah's Wife (Isaiah 8:1-4 and A_____ (Luke 2).

If you answered the above questions correctly then you are ready to go to the next level.
II Timothy 2:15

THE APOSTLE'S CHARGE

A charge to keep I have

A God to Glorify

Let every dying soul be Saved

And fitted for the sky

to serve this present day

A calling to Fulfill

All my strength engaged

To do the MASTER'S WILL!!!!

'Come into the

Prophetic

Flow. . . . .

And he gave GIFTS
UNTO MEN . . . . get ready to go

to the next level of revelation, Pray as you read, dangerous
revelation inside . . . Prophel Barsh D.Div.

WHO IS THE PROPHET?

Old Testament prophets voiced a particular way of looking at history and world events. They spoke as the mouthpieces of God, addressing his people and revealing to them his divine plan. They relate the address of God to his people through the processes of history. In admonishing the Israelites, calling them to repentance and redemption, the prophets stressed monotheism, morality, and messianism—themes carried forward into Christianity.

The Old Testament prophets are similar to figures in other cultures of the ancient Near East. In the earlier texts, figures such as Samuel are called not only prophet but seer. The seer knew the technical skills of divination and could predict the course of future events; the trade appears in various surrounding cultures. The prophets of the other nations were on occasion ecstatic figures -- persons who performed their tasks by whipping themselves into a state of ecstatic frenzy. Whether the Israelite prophets were influenced by or even participants in ecstatic prophecy is a subject of scholarly debate. Another facet of the same debate concerns the relationship of the Old Testament prophets to official institutions within the fabric of Israelite society. Some Old Testament prophets may have been cultic functionaries, and others, members of the royal court. Or they may have remained aloof from the institutional forms within which their counterparts in other cultures worked, free to develop criticism of cult or court according to the perception of the moment.

Old Testament prophets expressed their perception in a number of stereotyped forms of speech. One of the most common forms defines the prophetic message not simply as a word but also as an event: "The Word of the Lord came to me. . ." Also common to the prophets is their ability to intercede for their people. The prophets report their experiences of the call to action in a stereotyped form: commission, objection, reassurance. A typical form of prophetic speech is the oracle, or word from God, in which the expression of divine judgment is prefixed by an indictment that the prophet understands as his own explanation of cause for the divine judgment. In addition to the oracle of judgment, the prophet employs a divine promise for deliverance.

In Christian belief the Holy Spirit "spake through the (Old Testament) prophets." In the New Testament, prophesying, or ecstatic utterance, was regarded as a special gift bestowed on a select number of men and women. It was accorded great respect until the rise of MONTANISM in the 2nd century AD discredited it in the eyes of the orthodox. Thereafter, it was associated primarily with mystics and millenarians, people and sects that were often (but by no means always) labeled as heretical. Among Protestants the Anabaptists and Quakers stress the gift of prophecy. In Islam, MUHAMMAD is believed to be "the Seal of the Prophets," the last and greatest of God's human messengers.

Malachi 4:5-6 Behold I will send you Elijah the prophet before the coming of the great and dreadful day of the Lord, and he shall turn the heart of the fathers to the children, and the heart of the children to their fathers, lest I come and smite the earth with a curse!

We also read in the book of Proverbs that the CURSE cometh not without a CAUSE. The earth is cursed due to the lack of fathers. Where are the fathers is the cry of both, the world and the church. Notice Malachi said it would be a PROPHET who would do the RESTORING.

We have been in the midst of a reformation for over 500 years now and the church is PROGRESSIVELY been restored. The APOSTOLIC MOVEMENT is not a denomination, it is a people of purpose designed, predestined before the world began, ordained and ordered to usher in the MANIFESTED GLORY OF GOD TO THE FINAL GENERATION, those who no longer will be spectators but participants in bringing the CROWNING OF KING JESUS TO THE EARTH! THERE IS A CRY FOR WORSHIP, God is restoring truth, removing error, Restoring true covenant fathers and son relationships and removing the spirit of prostitution from the temple. God is restoring biblical protocol and removing religious Politics.

Restoration is a work of the Holy Spirit in the hearts of the believers and in the life of the church, therefore INTERCESSORS ARE TO RALLY AROUND THE ALTARS. This manual is not an exhaustive study, but an accuracy fresh study, 'THE SCHOOL OF THE PROPHETS'. Welcome to year 2001, New millennium, New generation, Age of restoration and reformation! BACK TO THE ORIGINAL. The author is not attempting to magnify or over emphasize the offices of the APOSTLE/PROPHET, but desire to emphasize what God is emphasizing in this time, it is an APOSTOLIC HOUR. For your blessings, this manual has been reviewed by major international apostles and prophets to ensure that it's accuracy, clarity and written in the spirit of truth.
  Come into the PROPHETIC AND APOSTOLIC FLOW!!!!

Prophet Barsh

WHO IS THE PROPHET?

The Prophet/Prophetess is one of the Five Fold Ascension gifts of Christ given to the church. (Ephesians 4:11, I Cor. 12:28; Acts 11:27, Acts 13:1).

The Greek meaning of Prophet: a foreteller, an inspired speaker, and a proclaimer of a divine message, denoted among the Greeks as an interpreter of the oracles of Gods.

The Septuagint meaning of Prophet: It is the translation of the word "Roeh" a seer, indicating that the prophet was one who had immediate intercourse with God. (I Sam. 9:9) It also translates the word "Nabhi" meaning either one in whom the message from God springs forth.

Amos, the Prophet speaks, God will do nothing, but reveals His secrets unto His servants the prophets. There is a prophetic movement happening in the church now without man's permission. The song of the Lord is returning to the temple, the ministry of the psalmist, prophet and minstrel is taking on a whole new dimension. Prophetic worship leaders will begin to mature the Body to get pass praise, enter into worship and move on into glory, beyond the veil, pageantry, art, dance and drama will now be a great part of worship, changing the traditional norm of services. We must be given to the spontaneous of the spirit to move in our worship through personal prophecy, corporate prophecy and allow the the presbytery to judge whatever is happening in the house. Churches will begin to examine their mode of worship. Move beyond their traditional upbringings, and enter fully in the obedience of this present truth of restoration of the apostolic order. The Prophets are the eyes of the church. The Apostle and the prophet is an office in the church. It is a governmental function. The church has been operating with incomplete foundations. God mentions five extension gifts to the Body of Christ. Notice He did not mention just the Pastor. Most churches operate with a one-man band, the pastor controlling every movement in the church. It is time out for the one-man solo. The prophetic ministry never competes; it completes what is lacking in the body. The Prophet works part of a team to discern the mind of Christ for the church. There are some realms, growth, and maturity the body will never get to without these two offices being restored to the Body of Christ. The question has been, will our church recognize the Apostle and Prophet? This is the New Testament Pattern. God has given the pattern. We must follow the Divine Pattern or the glory will depart and Icabod will be over the doorsteps. No matter how many members you have, God is tired of the sacrifices without obedience!!

The Prophet is the "Mouthpiece of God"; many believers move in some realm of the prophetic, but this does not mean they can call themselves a Prophet. The Prophet has to be proven by a proven seasoned Prophet. Jeremiah said, "God ordained me to be a Prophet before the foundations of the world. The calling of the prophet, then calls for a season of training, season of mentoring and a season of being in the School of the Prophets moving in the company of other seasoned prophets. That is why we conduct "The School of the Prophets". It is not just for Prophets but also, for those who desire to understand their spiritual gifts and discern the true from the false. That is why everything spoken in the house must be judged. The pastor's word must be judged; some are saying we must watch out for the prophet. Well you better check the teacher, the evangelist and the pastor. The ministry of the Prophet and the Apostle brings perfection, correction and maturity to the Body of Christ to flow in the fullness of Christ. That they may comprehend Christ in the length, the depth, the height and the breath!

The church has been behind time, God desires the church to get back on schedule with His divine timetable. It's a Prophetic hour of the church. We have not passed this way before, but it is time to change. Everybody will not change. Every church will not flow into the Apostolic/Prophetic realms. The church is a New Covenant of Believers, based on the revelation of Jesus Christ. I will build my church! The Church is not built on the revelation of man, neither is it built on man's tradition; it is built on the revelation of Jesus Christ.

The meaning of the word "Prophet" is the spokesman and the mouthpiece of God. God is always speaking, we must always be hearing. Hearing in the realms of the spirit. God said that Aaron would be Moses' "Prophet". Exodus 7:1; God said He would raise up a Prophet. He would put His words in his mouth and that the prophet would speak in His name, as His Ambassador. Though the Prophet is the general term for God's spokesman, in the Old Testament it appears the Prophet is also referred to as a seer. This appears in I Sam. 9:9; Man of God, I Sam. 9:6; Servant of God, and messenger of God.

In the Old Testament alone there are major and minor Prophets; Obadiah, Joel, Jonah, Amos, Hosea, Isaiah, Micah, Jeremiah, Zephaniah, Nahum, Habakkuk, Ezekiel, Haggai, Zechariah and Malachi.

The Ephesians were admonished that the church was built upon a foundation of Apostles and Prophets. Jesus Christ being the Chief Cornerstone. In the book of Acts, which is the Acts, the actions of the Apostles. The Apostles ordained elders to oversee the churches. Churches were never started by pastors these were prophets for their generation. We need modern day prophets who will speak the word of God. Regardless of man's persecution, Prophets will not bow to the witchcraft of Jezebel or to the tradition of man.

Prophets will not just prophesy money, but prophets will speak the truth. Most churches foundations have been laid improver. Most believers have no understanding of the Prophetic ministry. The Prophets are the eyes of the church. They give direction, confirmation, education, activation, consultation, revelation, and inspects foundations and doctrines, foundations and doctrines that have been deviating from the original purpose of God. The devil and his crowd hate the Prophets, so if you are a Prophet hater, then you know what crowd you identify with. The Prophet does not seek the approval of man neither does he/she seek their letters. Jesus did not get his credentials from the Sadducees; neither did He get ordained by the Pharisees of His day. The Prophets alert the church of damnable doctrines, which will weaken the power of the church. It is time we return to the 1st Century pattern of true biblical Apostolic church and order. It is time to get back on course and stay on course. Regardless of what comes God is tired of our rituals without purity. He is tired of our ceremonies without true covenant, tired of our choirs with Christ. But, God is rising up a people, His remnant who will pass the test, who will stand their ground and not bow to the persecutions that will try their faith.

THE SCHOOL OF THE PROPHETS/APOSTLES

WHO IS THE PROPHET?

That the eyes of your understanding being enlightened, that ye may know what is the hope and the calling and what the riches of the glory of his inheritance in the saints.... Ephesians 1:18

There is a glory that you are walking in now, but it is not all the glory that the Father has given you, that's why all that you know is being tested, you are probably under attack, just reading this manual means you are reaching for a greater revelation of yourself not for yourself, but for that which you love, your predestined purpose. You are ordained to walk in a greater glory, most churches large or small are walking in elementary stages of Christ, its time to grow up in Him. Be encouraged that the greatest hour of the church is on the horizon, if we suffer, we will reign! The devil is only after your glory!! He attacks your body, finances, and family to steal your glory... Be thou faithful unto death!! The persecution and struggle you are facing cannot be compared to the glory that is about to be revealed about you. You are God's number one interest for this generation, travail to birth what the Father has ordained you to birth. You are a part of God's hidden agenda, His battle troops, don't abort the mission, travail for the final generation!!!

Christ has an eternal plan and vision for His church that is greater than any single vision. We are progressively moving toward perfection, we must change and go from the glory of yesterday to the present glory that God wants to bestow upon His church. God doesn't remove what was done in the past. He desires to pour new wine in it to express a greater glory, then the priests can release a fresh glory for a fresh generation. Thank God for the past moves of the Spirit, thank God for the past fathers of past moves, but it is a new day, welcome the new fathers 'let's move on!!! It's a season change, we will survive this season change, God is stripping us of the old to put on the new. Then we can experience a fresh glory in our worship, songs, dance and praises and on our relationships. Therefore to grasp the wisdom of this book, be willing to place yourself, your vision, your methods, your ways and attitudes under the scrutiny of the Holy Spirit. Let not truth offend you, grow and change. We all must crucify our past. Our attitudes and negativism that has hindered the church. Jesus' prayer for His church is that we become one even as he and the Father are one.

Restoration is a term used to understand God is restoring that which was lost. What was lost? The divine order of his church and mandate. The apostle and prophet/prophetess is one of the five fold ascension gifts of Christ given to the church to restore, to reshape, to retrain leaders to release that which the devil used to retard the church! (Eph 4:11, I Cor 12:28, Acts 11:27, Acts 13:1). In Greek: Prophet means a foreteller, an inspired speaker, a proclaimer of a divine message, denoted among the Greeks as an interpreter of the oracles of God. In the Septuagint it is the translation of the Word "Roeh" a seer, indicating that the prophet was one who had immediate intercourse with God (I Sam 9:9) It also translates the word "Nabhi" meaning either 'One in whom the message from God springs forth. Amos, the prophet speaks, God will do nothing, but reveals his secrets unto his servants the prophets. There is a prophetic movement happening in the church now without man's permission, the song of the Lord is returning to the temple, the ministry of the Psalmist, Prophet and Minstrel is taking on a whole new dimension. Prophetic worship leaders will begin to mature the body to get past praise, enter into worship and move on into glory, beyond the veil, pageantry, art, dance and drama will now be a great part of worship, changing the traditional norm of services, we must be given to the spontaneity of the spirit to move in our worship through personal prophecy, corporate prophecy and allow the Presbytery to judge whatever is happening in the house. Churches will begin to examine their mode of worship, move beyond their traditional upbringings, and enter fully in the obedience of this present truth of restoration of the Apostolic order. The prophets are the eyes of the church.

The Apostle and the Prophet is an office in the church, in the coming move of God, the Apostle will not be someone who blows in and blows out. The Apostle/Prophet will be on the governing staff of Apostolic territorial governing churches. God is redefining our roles and restructuring leadership to get the church to the next level in Him. The Apostolic is a governmental function, with a governing anointing. The church has been operating with incomplete foundations, God mentions five extension gifts to the body of Christ, notice he did not mention just one, the pastor, most churches operate with a one man band, the pastor controlling every movement in the church, it's time out for the one man solo. The Apostolic and the prophetic ministry brings the church into maturity. It submits under true Biblical authority; it completes what's lacking in the body.

The Prophet works part of an Apostolic team to discern the mind of Christ for the church. The Apostle mainly deals to lay Biblical foundations and correct improper foundations, the Prophets point direction, helps the church adjust and survive certain season changes in the body. There are some realms, growth, maturity the body will never get to without these two offices being restored to the body of Christ. I warn you not to be intimidated by these gifts, God sent them to edify you, receive them, celebrate them before your congregation. Remember God did not call Adam to be alone. Most frustration of pastors comes due to fear of allowing others to touch the vision.

Most pastors walk in some realm of the Apostolic in gathering people together. This does not mean they are called as an Apostle. God is returning the true spirit of fathering in the body of Christ,

Malachi 4:6, and he shall turn the hearts of the fathers to the children's and the heart of the children to their fathers, lest I come and smite the earth with a curse.

There is a clarion call of true fathers to the house of God. God desires true sons and daughters who will be accountable and responsible to guard the seed of the house and develop character to transfer the legacy to the next generation.

The question has been, well our church does not recognize the Apostle/Prophet, God has given the pattern, we must follow divine pattern, or the glory will depart and Icabod will be over the doorposts, no matter how many members the church has, God is tired of the sacrifices without obedience!!

Lev 10:1, And Nadab and Ahihu, the sons of Aaron, took either of them his censer, and put fire therein, and put incense thereon and offered strange fire before the Lord, which he commanded not. 2. And there went out fire from the Lord and devoured them, and they died before the Lord.

These were sons of Eli who were being trained as priests who moved beyond their boundary, instituting an order not ordained in the house by God. They perceived because they were the blood sons of the priest they could do whatever they wanted, they broke spiritual protocol and were not restrained from working their witchcraft in the temple. Eli, the priest didn't correct his spiritual sons. Therefore he lost his priesthood ministry. The Apostolic is an introduction to what God is about to do, Restore his priesthood of the believers.

The Prophet is the 'mouthpiece of God', many believers move in some realm of the prophetic, but this does not mean they can call themselves a prophet, the prophet has to be proven by proven seasoned prophets. Jeremiah said, God ordained me to be a prophet before the foundation of the world!! The calling of the prophet, then calls for a season of training, season of mentoring and a season of being in the school of the prophets and moving in the company of other seasoned prophets. That's why we conduct the school of the prophets, it's for leaders to grasp present truth and activate the prophetic flow in their body and to understand their spiritual gifts and discern the true from the false. That's why everything spoken in the house must be judged. In the midst of truth, error can be released but not discerned by novices. This is why it's imperative to restore the offices of the Apostle and Prophet to the church. The tradition of man has weakened the power of the church. Many churches have a great following but are doctrinal in error. The early church was under a plurality of overseers who were the checks and balances of the body, never was lead by one overseer. The pastor's word must be judged, some are saying we must watch out for that prophet, well you better check the teacher, the prophet gives direction, confirmation, education, activation, consultation, revelation, and inspects foundations and doctrines, which have deviated from the original purposes of God. The devil and his crowd hate the prophets, so if you are a prophet hater, then you know what crowd you identify with. The prophet does not seek the approval of man; neither does he seek their letters. Jesus didn't get his credentials from the Sadducees; neither did he get ordained by the Pharisees of his day. The Prophet points the direction the church ought to be going, points the direction of what's next on God's agenda. The Prophets alerts the church of damnable doctrines which will weaken the power of the church. It's time we return to the 1st century pattern of true Biblical Apostolic church and Apostolic order. It's time to get back on course and stay the course, irregardless of what comes, God is tired of our rituals without relationships, he is tired of our preaching without purity, he is tired of our ceremonies without true covenants, tired of our choirs without Christ!!! But God is raising up a people, His remnant who will pass the test, who will stand their ground and not bow to the persecution which will try their faith.

Evangelist and the pastor. The ministry of the Prophet and the Apostle brings perfection, correction, and maturity to the body to flow in the fullness of Christ, that all may comprehend Christ in the length, the depth the height and the breadth!! The church has been behind time, God desires we get on schedule with His divine timetable. It's a prophetic hour of the church. We have not passed this way before, but it's time to change. Everybody will not change; every church will not flow into the Apostolic/Prophetic realms. The church is a new covenant of believers, based on the revelation of Jesus Christ, I will build my church!!! The church is not built on the revelation of man, neither is it built on man's tradition, it is built on the revelation of Jesus Christ. The meaning of the word 'Prophet', "thy spokesman", the mouthpiece of God, as one saying God is always speaking, we must be always hearing, hearing in the realms of the spirit. God said that Aaron would be Moses' 'Prophet', Exodus 7:1, God said He would raise up a prophet, (a prophetic people who will be a prophetic voice to the nations). He would put His words in his mouth and that the prophet would speak in His name, as His ambassador. Though the prophet is the general term for God's spokesman, in the Old Testament it appears, the prophet is also referred to as a seer. This appears in I Sam 9:9, man of God, I Sam 9:6, servant of God, and messenger of God. In the Old Testament alone there are major and minor prophets, Obadiah, Joel, Jonah, Amos, Hosea, Isaiah, Micah, Jeremiah, Zephaniah, Nahum, Habbakkuk, Ezekiel, Haggai, Zechariah, and Malachi.

The Ephesians were admonished that the church was built upon a foundation of Apostles and Prophets, Jesus Christ being the Chief Cornerstone. In the Book of Acts, which is the actions of the Apostles, the apostles ordained elders to oversee the churches, churches were never started by pastors. These were prophets for there generation, we need modern day prophets who will speak the word of god, irregardless of man's persecution. Prophets who will not bow to the witchcraft of Jezebel tradition of man, prophets who will not just prophesy money, but prophets who will speak truth. Most churches foundations have been laid improper.

Most believers have no understanding of the prophetic ministry. This hunger must be fulfilled through true prophetic mandate or we will see many believers calling on psychics and not the prophets. The prophet is the eyes of the church.

PRESBYTERY OF THE CHURCH

The scripture gives the divine pattern of the ordination of those to be separated unto ministry. In the Old Testament the anointing oil was only used to anoint one into an office, or to separate unto ministry.

I Timothy 4:14 , neglect not the gift that is in thee, which was given thee by prophecy with the laying on of the hands of the Presbytery. We see that laying on of hands was a practice of the early church to impart spiritual gifts, not just casting out demons. Notice also, Numbers 27:18, and the Lord said unto Moses, take thee Joshua the son of Nun, a man in whom is the Spirit and lay hands upon him; hands were laid upon Joshua because he had already been proven in his calling, and Moses did as the Lord commanded him, and he took Joshua and set him before Eleazar the priest, and before the congregation, and laid his hands upon him and gave him a charge, as the Lord commanded him.

A 'Presbytery' is one of the 5-fold governmental ministries in the Body of Christ. It speaks into the life of those set apart for ministry. A team of proven gifted leaders. The Presbytery should be ordained elders, one of proven character, morals, integrity and in covenant with the body. The persons receiving the Presbytery as well as releasing needs a spirit of expectancy and in an attitude of worship. One should not approach the Presbytery with a predetermined agenda. They should be open to the voice of God. Many have stood before the Prophets and Presbytery and voiced that the words did not confirm with their spirit. The word of the prophets is not to confirm with your spirit, it is to confirm with the word of the Lord! You will not receive either from a Prophet or a Presbytery with a predetermined agenda. We believe the time will come that those who desire marriage in the house of God, will first go before the Presbytery to confirm their marriage. Many marriages are born out of lust and not out of covenant.

The Presbytery are called to ordain ministers, elders, consecrate Bishops, release ministries, activate gifts, speak destinys, confirm gifts, correct error, establish the church in the true Biblical pattern.

TRUE VS FALSE PROPHETS

Both the Old and New Testaments abound with evidences and warnings against false prophets. Whenever there are true prophets, Satan will stir up false prophets in order to deceive people. Here are 12 tests to apply to all prophets:

1. <u>Test the Spirit:</u> (I John 4:1-3) Is it the Holy Spirit, the human spirit or an evil spirit that is giving the utterance?

2. <u>Test of Fulfillment</u> (Deut. 18:22) Does the prophetic word come to pass or not? Time is the great prover of prophecies.

3. <u>Test of Worship</u> (Deut. 13: 1-5) Does the prophetic word lead us to worship God, or lead us away from the true God?

4. <u>Test of Doctrines</u> (I John 4:1-6; I Tim 4:1-3; Isa 18:19-20) Do the prophets speak in harmony with the major doctrines of redemption? Do they speak according to the sound doctrine of God's Word?

5. <u>Test of Fruit:</u> (Matt 7:15-23) What is the fruit of the prophet's lifestyle? It is by their fruits - not by their gifts - that we shall know them.

6. <u>Test of Covetousness:</u> (Micah 3:11, II Pet 2:1-3) Are these prophets making merchandise of the people of God? We will know false prophets by their love of money.

7. <u>Test of Ministry to the People:</u> (Jer 23:18-23) Do these prophets turn the people from their sinful lifestyle to God? Without holiness of life none shall see the Lord (Heb 12: 7 - 14)

8. <u>Test of Humility:</u> (I Cor. 8:1) Does the prophetic word produce humility or pride in our hearts? Does it exalt the person or Christ? Does it create hunger and thirst and love in us for the living God?

9. <u>Test of Value</u>: While we are to "fight the good fight" by the prophecies that go before us (I Tim. 1:18), do we value the infallible Word of God above the person's prophetic words? Most prophetic words are confirmed, on a personal basis, what the inspired and infallible Word has already told us to do on a general basis.

10. <u>Test of Confirmation:</u> Is the prophetic utterance confirmation to our spirits? Does it agree with the already known and revealed will of God? Is there the rule of peace in our hearts? If not, we must seek the counsel of proven ministry.

PRESBYTERY OF THE CHURCH

The scripture gives the divine pattern of the ordination of those to be separated unto ministry. In the Old Testament the anointing oil was only used to anoint one into an office, or to separate unto ministry.

I Timothy 4:14 , neglect not the gift that is in thee, which was given thee by prophecy with the laying on of the hands of the Presbytery. We see that laying on of hands was a practice of the early church to impart spiritual gifts, not just casting out demons. Notice also, Numbers 27:18, and the Lord said unto Moses, take thee Joshua the son of Nun, a man in whom is the Spirit and lay hands upon him; hands were laid upon Joshua because he had already been proven in his calling, and Moses did as the Lord commanded him, and he took Joshua and set him before Eleazar the priest, and before the congregation, and laid his hands upon him and gave him a charge, as the Lord commanded him.

A 'Presbytery' is one of the 5-fold governmental ministries in the Body of Christ. It speaks into the life of those set apart for ministry. A team of proven gifted leaders. The Presbytery should be ordained elders, one of proven character, morals, integrity and in covenant with the body. The persons receiving the Presbytery as well as releasing needs a spirit of expectancy and in an attitude of worship. One should not approach the Presbytery with a predetermined agenda. They should be open to the voice of God. Many have stood before the Prophets and Presbytery and voiced that the words did not confirm with their spirit. The word of the prophets is not to confirm with your spirit, it is to confirm with the word of the Lord! You will not receive either from a Prophet or a Presbytery with a predetermined agenda. We believe the time will come that those who desire marriage in the house of God, will first go before the Presbytery to confirm their marriage. Many marriages are born out of lust and not out of covenant.

The Presbytery are called to ordain ministers, elders, consecrate Bishops, release ministries, activate gifts, speak destinys, confirm gifts, correct error, establish the church in the true Biblical pattern.

DIVINATION

Divination is moving in the spirit realm without official authorization of the government of God in the local church.

The psychic moves under a familiar spirit of witchcraft, foreign to the government of God, not authorized by Jesus Christ. Anyone involved with this spirit will incur the curse. I Chronicles 10:13-14, "So Saul died for his transgression which he committed against the Lord, even against the word of the Lord which he kept not, and also for asking counsel of one that had a familiar spirit, to enquire of it; and enquired not of the Lord: therefore he slew him, and turned the kingdom unto David the son of Jesse." The curse does not come without a cause!

Pharaoh consulted the magicians of Egypt, Saul consulted the witch of Endor; America is bombarded with Palm Readers, Psychic Hotlines, Connections and TV shows. Acts 20:28-30, "Take heed therefore unto yourselves and to all the flock, over which the Holy Ghost hath made you overseers, to feed the church of God, which he hath purchased with his own blood. For I know this, that after my departing shall grievous wolves enter in among you, not sparing the flock. Also of your ownselves shall men arise, speaking perverse things, to draw away disciples after them.

It is time to put the psychics out of business. It is time for he church to move to Kingdom and transfer the wealth the psychics are taking back to its rightful place, "THE CHURCH". The psychic is a perverted seducing spirit of witchcraft. It is an illegal entry to the revelation of God. Stop calling the psychic now! Repent of this sin! There is someone else in the empire! the Elijah type prophets and apostles are coming out of the cave!

PROPHESY!!!

PROPHETIC WORD TO THE NATION

"Get ready people of the earth. Whole systems, government structures, religious structures are about to be shaken from their very foundations.

I the Lord only will be exalted. I will not share my glory with another. I am about to do a new thing. Prepare for change. Great calamities will come upon the earth and the nations.

USA, your chest will be deflated, once again you will receive calluses on your knees. I will shake denominational walls. I will make my people one. A greater glory shall be released. Get ready for the Greater Glory.

Many of you have sat in the valley of tradition and indecision. Now the hour has come God will interrupt man's religious order and agenda and establish a new order to usher in change!

Change is on the horizon, revival will break in the early spring, watch for the hurricanes and earthquakes. Spiritual alliances and bridges will collapse signifying I am tired of old structures, give way to the new.

The spirit of witchcraft shall be destroyed in your cities. Come away in the spirit and I will even show you a greater thing. Only as you stay in intersession will you bring down the dark prince over your nations.

Come away from your Temples! Visit the streets and then you will witness my hand bringing restoration and healing! Churches will merge in the inner city, unity shall be the key to deliverance. Financial institutions will collapse, now prepare yourself, your families, seek my face, get financially secure, trust in my hand, watch governmental control, communism shall creep into the USA, weep at the altars, weep at the altars saith the Spirit of Truth.

PSYCHIC HOTLINE/PROPHET HOTLINE?

"I Samuel 28:1-9, And it came to pass in those days, that the Philistines gathered their armies together for warfare, to fight with Israel. And Achish said unto David, Know thou assuredly, that thou shalt go out with me to battle, thou and thy men.And David said to Achish, Surely thou shalt know what thy servant can do. And Achish said to David, Therefore will I make thee keeper of mine head for ever. Now Samuel was dead, and all Israel had lamented him, and buried him in Ramah, even in his own city. And Saul had put away those that had familiar spirits, and the wizards, out of the land. And the Philistines gathered themselves together, and came and pitched in Shunem: and Saul gathered all Israel together, and they pitched in Gilboa. And when Saul saw the host of the Philistines, he was afraid, and his heart greatly trembled. And when Saul enquired of the Lord, the Lord answered him not, neither by dreams, nor by Urim, nor by prophets. Then said Saul unto his servants, Seek me a woman that hath a familiar spirit, that I may go to her, and enquire of her. And his servants said to him, Behold, there is a woman that hath a familiar spirit at Endor. And Saul disguised himself, and put on other raiment, and he went, and two men with him, and they came to the woman by night: and he said, I pray thee, divine unto me by the familiar spirit, and bring me him up, whom I shall name unto thee. And the woman said unto him, Behold, thou knowest what Saul hath done, how he hath cut off those that have familiar spirits, and the wizards, out of the land: wherefore then layest thou a snare for my life, to cause me to die?

This is the hour of restoration. God is restoring his Divine order and pattern of the New Testament Church. this manual is designed for the serious student of the word who desires to go beyond salvation; renting the veil of traditional thought moving into their predestined purpose which the Father ordained before the foundations of the world.

God through supernatural ministry of the Apostle and prophet will loose the seals of your life, thereby you will walk as Jesus in the flesh, demonstrating the power of God, fulfilling the purpose of

Jehovah..

This manual is for the believer who has been destroyed for the lack of knowledge (Gnosis) "full knowledge", Jesus desires for you to come into. The full wisdom, full depth and full comprehension of Jesus Christ's ministry, manifesting in 5 dimension, 5 offices, and 5 supernatural gifts to the church.

This manual will also allow churches to have study sessions of this Apostolic/Prophetic mantle offices. Today we cannot turn on our television without hearing about the Psychic Friends Networks, Psychic Connections and Psychic Hotlines.

The Spirit of Witchcraft has bombarded the air waves. Many believers who lack prophetic insight and prophetic leadership become discouraged that their dreams and visions are not coming to pass and get caught up in a psychic grip, a demonic curse by dialing 1-900 PSYCHIC. We need a <u>Prophetic Hotline</u>! We need a <u>Prophet Connection!, A Prophet Network</u>! The psychic hotlines releases the spirit of witchcraft, causes spirit addictions to a warlock and witch who have went illegally in the backdoor stealing revelation and truth not exalting the Lordship of Jesus Christ.

When the body of Christ gets wisdom on the Apostolic/Prophetic gifts, we will put the psychics out of business. God is raising up a people who will form a prophetic network and not compromise, neither negotiate with the false prophets of Baal.

this manual guarantees to bring you into clarity and balance. You will never be the same again. Let him that hath an ear, hear what the Spirit saith to the church. Instead of seeking a familiar spirit (witch of endor) seek the Prophet.

Scripture References:

Deuteronomy 18:9-14
I Samuel 15:23
Galatians 3:1
I Samuel 9:3-7

WE NEED A PROPHET!

The prophet is the "mouthpiece" of God, the voice of liberation.

When we fail to hear the prophets, then the psychic will speak. It is time the true prophets arise and stop the demonic onslaught of witchcraft in our nation.

The devil hates the prophet because they bring the revelation of Jesus Christ to the people. Prophets bring restoration. The purpose of restoration is to bring the church back to its original pattern. Because of the traditions of man and the religious system, the church has deviated off course. It is time to return to the original pattern of the New Testament Church.

God has set 5 offices in His church. It is time the Body of Christ receive the office of the Apostle and Prophet. The prophet is the eyes of the Body. the prophet brings clarity, the prophet sees, the prophet points to the next agenda on God's timetable. The prophet alerts the church of damnable doctrines that will weaken the power of the church.

Many have deviated into the New Age Philosophy, deviated into tradition, deviated into eastern occults, deviated into mushing. Hear Jesus! If it does not exalt Christ and confess Him as Lord, it is a damnable religion and cursed. The Holy Ghost says don't even bid them God's Speed.

PURPOSE OF THE PROPHET

Jesus is involved in the restoration of His church. Each of us is being compelled to look beyond our personal and local ministry goals and catch a glimpse of Christ's vision for his whole Church and the nations of the world. The saints are having to rise above natural limitations accept "restoration assignments" as King Jesus issues His orders.

The Westcoast Annual Prophetic Congresses has been birthed in response to such orders. Our desire is to help usher in Apostles and Prophets as Foundation Ministries in the church as well as train and activate all Five-fold Ministries and facilitate the full restoration of presently restored truth and practice.

In Ephesians 4:8 and 11, we read that Jesus gave the Five-fold Ministries as gifts to the church. "And He gave some Apostles and some Prophets, and some Evangelists, and some Pastors and Teachers." These ministry gifts are dear to the heart of God. They are key to His plan. The Apostle and Prophet are paramount to building the foundation of the church. "You are being built upon the foundation of Apostles and Prophets. Jesus Christ Himself being Chief Cornerstone." Ephesians 2:20

In talking about ministry gifts, Paul goes on in verse 12 and 13 to write that the purpose of Spiritual gifts are "For the equipping of the saints for the work of service to the building up of the Body of Christ; until we all attain to the unity of the faith, and of the knowledge of the Son of God, to mature man, to the measure of the statue which belongs to the fullness of Christ."

God is currently bringing forth a company of Five-fold Ministers; literally thousands who will help prepare the way for Christ's second coming. These men and women of destiny are to be voices to the Church and to nations. They call forth Apostles and Prophets of power and restoration who will help bring the Church to unity and maturity. They are to function in the elijah anointing that god placed on John the Baptist to "make ready a people" and "prepare the way for Christ's coming".Isa. 40:3, Mal. 4:5, Mt. 3:3, Luke 1:76

Many things must yet come into order. Jesus desires to return, but according to His Word. He has given mandates regarding His Second Coming. As the people of god we must do our part to grow up in all aspects into Him.

According to Ephesians 4:11, God established 5 offices in His church to bring the church into perfection, fullness, maturity, balance and divine order. God has set some in the church, some Apostles, some Prophets, some Evangelists, some Pastors and Teachers.

II Corinthians 12:28, God has set some in the church "Ekklesia" (called out ambassadors, mouthpiece of the King) first Apostles, secondarily Prophets.

Matthew speaks of the first shall be last and the last shall be first. God is restoring divine order, restoring first things. Foundations have to be restored, structures must be build on proper foundations.

The early church apostles and prophets walked in demonstration and power. Apostle Paul speaks boldly in I Corinthians 1:1-5; "And I, brethren, when I came to you, came not with excellency of speech or of wisdom, declaring unto you the testimony of God. For I determined not to know anything among you, save Jesus Christ, and him crucified. And I was with you in weakness, and in fear, and in much trembling. And my speech and my preaching was not with enticing words of man's wisdom, but in demonstration of the Spirit and of power. That your faith should not st and in the wisdom of men, but in the power of god." They preached Christ and Him crucified.

God is using the School of the Prophets to bring forth a company of Apostles and Prophets; trained and anointed to stand before Presidents, Mayors and Prime Ministers and speak to the nations.

The Elijah type prophets are coming out of the cave. Prophesy prophets, Prophesy!

The School of the Prophets is to train, activate and educate all those who will participate in ushering in ultimately the crowning of Jesus Christ. Being a voice, a forerunner for the final age, the Apostolic Age. An age of even greater power, greater miracles, greater prosperity, greater demonstration to stop the spirit of witchcraft and establish God's people as a force in the earth.

CHAPTER ONE

God's Government - 5 Fold Ministry Gifts to the Church

1. God gave gifts unto men. Ephesians 4:11
   I Samuel 17:40, 5 tried stones

2. Jesus manifested Himself in 5 dimensions to bring the Church into fullness, perfection, completion, maturity and equipped to usher in the Kingdom.

3. Church - Kingdom Matthew 16:18
   Jesus preached Kingdom

4. 5-fold Government Officials.
   Ambassadors of the Kingdom, Sent ones, Legislate Policy, Establish rule and reign, Enforce covenant, learn Diplomatic Procedures in Diplomatic Chambers, Acts 2:47, Acts 20:28

5. Make disciples not prophets. Disciples become servants become Prophets.

6. 22 gifts in the body of Christ.

Next chapter, we will discover these gifts and activate them.

CHAPTER ONE STUDY QUESTIONS

God's government - 5 Fold Ministry Gifts to the Church

1. What does the word "Government"mean in the Greek?

2. Find in the gospels where Jesus was manifested as the Apostle, Prophet, evangelist, Pastor and Teacher.

3. What does the word "Ambassador" mean?

4. Have you identified your spiritual gifts?

5. Name me the 5-fold ministry extension gifts and offices of the church.

6. Name the 9 ways Christ manifested Himself to his church.

7. Should these office gifts and nine gifts still be operating today in every church? If so, why aren't they?

8. Define the word "Prophet".

CHAPTER TWO
ACTIVATE THE GIFTS
Romans 1:11, I Timothy 1:6

1. The gift of Prophecy. Romans 12:6 and I Corinthians 12:10
2. The gift of Ministering. Romans 12:7
3. The gift of Teaching. Romans 12:7
4. The gift of Exhortation. Romans 12:8
5. The gift of Giving. Romans 12:8
6. The gift of Ruling. romans 12:8
7. The gift of Mercy. Romans 12:8
9. The gift of the Word of Knowledge. I Corinthians 12:8
10. The gift of Faith. I Corinthians 12:9
11. The gift of Healing. I Corinthians 12:9
12. The gift of Miracles. I Corinthians 12:10
13. The gift of Discerning of spirits. I Corinthians 12:10
14. The gift of Tongues. I Corinthians 12:10
15. The gift of interpretation of Tongues. I Corinthians 12:10
16. The gift of Helps. I Corinthians 12:29
17. The gift of Governments. I Corinthians 12:28
18. The gift of the Apostle. I Corinthians 12:28 and Ephesians 4:11
19. The gift of the Prophet. I Corinthians 12:28 and Ephesians 4:11
20. The gift of the Evangelist. Ephesians 4:11
21. The gift of the Pastor. Ephesians 4:11
22. The gift of the Teacher. I Corinthians 12:28 and Ephesians 4:11

Jesus Christ gave gifts to men to edify His church. Nine (9) manifestations of the Holy Spirit, manifesting Himself nine (9) different ways in the Body of Christ.

Then there are the five (5) governmental office extension gifts given to the Body of Christ. We need all five (5) grace office gifts to come into the fullness of Christ's full statue and comprehension, that we may know Christ in the length, depth, height and breadth.

Three (3) gifts of power that do something, three (3) gifts of revelation that reveals and three (3) gifts of utterance that speak. Each believer in the church has gifts that need to be identified, turned on, and released to edify the church.

CHAPTER TWO STUDY QUESTIONS

1. Apostle Paul speaks to Timothy to stir up the gift. How do we do this?

2. Write down and discuss your spiritual gifts.

3. How are the gifts to operate in the church?

4. Should prophets prophesy on the telephone, in the parking lot, in the barroom?

5. Discuss the 9 manifestations of the office gifts and spiritual gifts and how they are to operate in the church.

6. When gifts are not operating, then religious politics, the spirit of witchcraft, and entertainment take the place of the Holy Ghost.

7. How often do you fast?

8. What does the word "Activate" mean?

CHAPTER THREE

THE PURPOSE OF THE SCHOOL & COMPANY OF PROPHETS

II Kings 5:8, Ezra 5:1, I Samuel 3:11, Isaiah 9:6, Amos 3:7, Daniel 1:22

1. Solid Leadership, New Testament Pattern, Establish House of God. Gather, Train, Build covenant Church City.

2. Raise up an army. Elijah type prophets. Usher in Jesus Christ. Confront the spirit of witchcraft.

3. Prophets need training and mentors.

4. Prophets are a governmental function. I Corinthians 12:28

5. Jeremiah 1:6 Ordained, trained, prepared, separated, released. Acts 13.

6. You don't choose Spiritual Fathers, God does.

7. David went from back of desert to Prophet, Priest and King.

8. 5 Training schools: Ramah, Bethel, Gilgal, Jericho and Jordan. I Samuel 19:18

9. School of the prophets - Elijah II Kings 2:9

10. Company of the Prophets - Samuel

11. Prophets are ordained Elders. Acts 13:1

12. Sons of the Prophets: Key - Servants

13. Promise Keeper - Prophetic Drama. Restoration of fathers to home and to the church. "Order in the Court"

CHAPTER THREE STUDY QUESTIONS

Purpose of the School and Company of Prophets

1. How does a Prophet become a prophet? Jeremiah 1:9

2. Who did Samuel, the Prophet, place in charge as in King? Who anointed David as King? who spoke to King David about the wife of Uriah the Hitite?

3. What is the purpose of the School of the Prophets?

4. Who is your Spiritual Father? covering authority of your life?

5. Who is the Prophet to your city? I Samuel 9:6

6. Who was over the School of the Prophets?

7. Who was over the Company of the Prophets?

CHAPTER FOUR

THE SET MAN PRINCIPLE
Building the Local Church Effectively

Acts 21:19, Numbers 27:16

1. God has set some in the body. I Corinthians 12

2. God sets the Set man (Marriage)

3. Set Man sets Teams - Jesus chose Twelve Matthew 10

4. Set man commands the team. Matthew 10

5. Set Man delegates to the team.

6. Teams understands role, function and anointing.

7. Set Man establishes set areas to reach.

8. Set Man selected inner three. Galatians 2:9

9. 3-12-Masses -----------> As one voice.

10. Set Man given to prayer.

11. Set Man must have love for the city. Nehemiah 1:3

12. True Bishops begin to organize people, educate them, feed them impart to their lives, raise them. Exodus 2:19

13. Teams must run and celebrate the vision. Habbabuk 2:9

14. Teams must finance the vision.

CHAPTER FOUR STUDY QUESTIONS

Set Man Principle

1. Jesus had a team of 12 disciples who were the foundational Apostles. Name them.

2. What does the word "Apostle" mean?

3. Jesus is our pattern, Lord and example. Name Jesus' inner circle.

4. What institution have your area Bishops established beside a church?

5. What is the purpose of a team?

6. What is your purpose on your leadership team?

7. What is the Jethro Principle?

8. How can you support your Set Man?

9. Is cleaning the Set Man's house, mowing the lawn or keeping the children a part of help ministry?

10. What should you do if your spiritual government is in sin?

11. What should you do if you are in leadership and another leader speaks negative of the Set Man, the Vision?

12. What is the protocol of your local assembly if a believer thinks spiritual government is out of control; scripture challenge.

13. What is your Set Man's Vision?

14. Your dreams will come to pass when you fulfill your Set Man's vision. Two visions in one house = division.

CHAPTER FIVE

APOSTOLIC AGE (REFORM)

1. Apostles are God's Ambassadors.

2. The Apostle is first in rank. They lay the foundation.

3. The Apostle can touch all other gifts.

4. The Apostle is often misunderstood.

5. Jesus cannot come until!!!! Acts 3:9

6. Apostles/Prophets are sent to geographical regions. Jeremiah 29:5-7

7. Apostles/Prophets change climates.

8. Apostles/Prophets change atmospheres.

9. Apostles/Prophets are hated by religious systems.

10. Apostles/Prophets establishes churches.

11. Apostles/Prophets move in supernatural anointing, signs, wonders, and miracles.

12. The Apostolic spirit is a pioneering spirit; pulling down religious error, flowing through prayer, planting truth in a region, changing geographical powers and establishing new powers and rules. Advancing the Kingdom of God.

13. The Apostolic spirit is a pioneering spirit; pulling down religious error, flowing through prayer, planting truth in a region, changing geographical powers and establishing new powers and rules. Advancing the Kingdom of God.

I Corinthians 4:9-15
I Corinthians 1:1, Galatians 1:1
II Corinthians 1:1, Galatians 1:1
Ephesians 1:1, Colossians 1:1

CHAPTER FIVE STUDY QUESTIONS

Apostolic Age (Reform)

1. Why would the local church need a map of their city?

2. Find the scripture in reference to Paul the Apostle from I Corinthians to Colossians.

3. What does laying on of hands have to do with the apostles?

4. Who is authorized to lay hands in the local church?

5. What is the purpose of the Presbytery?

6. What is the purpose of laying on of hands?

7. Describe the difference from the right hand, left hand and both hands?

8. Should believers be involved with reading the Horoscope, Zodiac, Tarot Cards, Palm readers?

9. Leviticus 10 speaks of Aaron's sons offering up "strange fire". What is strange fire?

CHAPTER SIX

PROPHETS PIONEERING ANOINTING

Romans 1:11, Ephesians 2:20

Pioneer Spirit to plow up
Pioneer Anointing to pull down
Pioneer Anointing to penetrate through
Pioneer Anointing to throw down
Pioneer Anointing to root out
Pioneer Anointing to endure season changes

IMPART

1. Location to establish truth. (bind, loose Matthew 16:19)

2. Pioneer discerns spiritual strongholds, spiritual climates, and spiritual atmospheres.

3. Pioneer builds a people to stand before t he territorial demonic council through prayer, fasting, and faithfulness. A people that will overthrow the plans. (breakthrough)

4. Pioneer must destroy the spirit of witchcraft, the controlling spirit over the minds of the people.

5. Apostle means "sent one". Sent to a particular people, region, Sent to pull down, plow up, plant ----> Authority, official seal of the government of God.

6. Prophets move beyond simple gift of prophecy such as comfort, exhort and edification. Prophets move in the realms of:

1. Correction	6. Revelation	11. Insight
2. Impartation	7. Consultation	12. Direction
3. Restoration	8. Illumination	13. Instruction
4. Demonstration	9. Education	14. Apostolic Loosing
5. Activation	10. Re-alignment	15. Apostolic Binding

CHAPTER SIX STUDY QUESTIONS

Prophet's Pioneering Anointing

1. Define Pioneer?

2. What is the Spirit of Witchcraft?

3. Who was Paul, the Apostle, sent to and Peter the Apostle sent to?

4. What is your local church Pastor pioneering now?

5. If the local church Pastor is not gifted to move in the prophetic, what can he do?

6. Is a person who prophecies, a prophet/prophetess?

7. Identify Satan's stronghold in your inner city?

CHAPTER SEVEN

MINSTREL, PSALMIST, & PROPHET

Song of the Lord to the House

1. God is doing a new thing, new day, new generation. Isaiah 41:13

2. You must have the Spirit of Issachar. II Chronicles 20:26

3. David brought the Ark up shouting.

4. David represents new order, new sound.

5. David brought song back to the House of God.

6. New glory shall be greater than the former.

7. New guard needs new instructors.

8. Joshua differed from Moses.

9. Prophet, Psalmists and minstrels must merge.

10. All those who are a part of the new order walk under authority.

11. Elijah received a double portion of Elisha's spirit. Understood his season, his master.

12. There is a new song for a new order.

13. You will become what you sing.

14. Davidic company sings the Psalms.

15. Stop singing tradition.

16. Musicians must be transformed to minstrel.

17. Soloist must be transformed to Psalmist.

18. New songs will create a new atmosphere

19. Spiritual climates will change when the Prophet/Psalmist/Minstrel are married.

CHAPTER SEVEN STUDY QUESTIONS

Minstrel, Psalmist and Prophet

1. The Ark is a symbolism of what?

2. What is the Spirit of Isschar?

3. Moses' administration and Joshua's administration, how do they differ?

4. Why is the Song of the Lord in the House of God so important?

5. What types of things are going on in your church leadership to prepare future leadership?

6. What is your church's 5 year vision plan?

7. How does the Saul administration differ from David's administration?

8. Whose administration are you submitted to?

9. Elijah said, "Bring me a _____ "

10. Minstrels tap into realms of the spirit that the devil hates and allows the prophet to prophesy at a higher level and unction.

11. You cannot prophesy above your revelation of truth.

CHAPTER EIGHT

PROPHETHOOD

Webster defines the word "hood"as a covering for the head and neck, sometimes the face. A hood is something one wars properly.

1. A Prophet can be a voice to the local assembly, voice to the city, voice to the state and nation. God determines the jurisdiction of the prophet.

2. Religious systems hate the Prophetic. Revelations 1:9

3. Jezebel is in the vicinity of every Prophet.

4. Spirit of Delilah is more deadly to the prophet versus Jezebel.

5. Prophethood speaks to the government.

6. Geographical regions, atmospheres, and climates will change because of the Prophet.

7. Revelations 12:17, The serpent will try to harass and intimidate the Prophet to abort the assignment.

8. The Prophet must not be controlled by the <u>"religioushood"</u>.

CHAPTER NINE

THE PROPHETESS

1. The Prophetess is a female prophet, ordained Elder who operates in governmental functions.

2. A Prophetess must be submitted to the Senior Pastor, to fulfill his vision.

3. The prophetess must teach others how to move in protocol toward leadership.

4. The Prophetess must agree with the Prophet.

5. The Prophetess must know her boundary of authority.

6. The Prophetess must serve the local church.

7. The prophetess must be an intercessor and teach others how to bring forth dreams and visions.

8. The Prophetess must be an armor bearer for the Prophet and his wife.

Scripture References:

Exodus 15:20

Judges 4:4

I Samuel 2:1-10

Isaiah 8:23

II Kings 22:14

Luke 2:36

CHAPTER 10

MINISTRY OF THE SEER

1. God has established the office of the Seer.

2. The Seer sees and only seeks in the ears of the Prophet or Pastor.

3. The Prophet declares to the Body.

4. The Seer has to walk in great humility after discerning great truth.

5. Seers establish intercession in the House of God.

6. Seers see for the Set Man and stop Satan's invasion.

7. A Seer without walking in authority becomes a loud mouth prophet.

I Samuel 9:9

> (Formerly in Israel, if a man went to inquire of God, he would say, "Come Let us go to the seer" because the prophet of today used to be called a seer)

I Samuel 9:11

> As they were going up the hill to the town, they met some girls coming out to draw water, and they asked them, Is the seer here?

I Samuel 9:19

> I am the seer, Samuel replied, Go up ahead of me to the high place, for today you are to eat with me, and in the morning I will let you go and will tell you all that is in your heart.

II Samuel 15:27

> The king also said to Zadok the priest, Aren't you a seer? Go back to the city in peace with your son Ahimaaz and

Jonathan son of Abiathar, You and Abiathar take your two sons with you.

II Samuel 24:11

Before David got up the next morning, the word of the Lord had come to Gad the prophet, David's seer.

I Chronicles 9:22

Altogether, those chosen to be gate keepers at the thresholds numbered 212. They were registered by genealogy in their villages. The gatekeepers had been assigned to their positions of trust by david and Samuel the seer.

I Chronicles 21:9

The Lord said to Gad, David's seer.

I Chronicles 25:5

All these were sons of Heman the king's seer. They were given him through the promises of God to exalt him. God gave Heman fourteen sons and three daughters.

I Chronicles 26:28

And everything dedicated by Samuel the seer and by Saul son of Kish, Abner son of Ner and Joab son of Zeruiah, and all the other dedicated things were in the care of Shelomith and his relatives.

I Chronicles 29:29

As for the events of King David's reign, from beginning to end, they ar written in the records of Samuel the Seer, the records of Nathan the prophet and the records of Gad the Seer.

II Chronicles 9:29

As for the other events of Solomon's reign, from beginning to end, are they not written in the records of Nathan the prophet, in the prophecy of Ahijah the Shilonite and in the visions of Iddo the seer concerning Jeroboam son of Nebat?

II Chronicles 12:15

As for the events of Rehoboam's reign, from beginning to end, are they not written in the records of Shemaiah the prophet and of Iddo the seer that deal with genealogies? There was continual warfare between Rehoboam and Jeroboam.

II Chronicles 16:7

At that time Hanani the seer came to Asa king of Judah and said to him: "Because you relied on the king of Aram and not on the Lord your God, the army of the king of Aram has escaped from your hand.

II Chronicles 16:10

Asa was angry with the seer because of this; he was so enraged that he put him in prison. At the same time Asa brutally oppressed some of the people.

II Chronicles 19:2

Jehu the seer, the son of Hanani, went out to meet him and said to the king, Should you help the wicked and love those who hate the Lord? Because of this, the wrath of the Lord is upon you.

II Chronicles 29:25

He stationed the Levites in the temple of the Lord with cymbals, harps and lyres in the way prescribed by David and Gad the king's seer and Nathan the prophet this was commanded by the Lord through his prophets.

II Chronicles 29:30

King Hezekiah and his officials ordered the Levites to praise the Lord with the word of David and of Asaph the seer. So they sang praises with gladness and bowed their heads and worshipped.

II Chronicles 35:15

> The musicians, the descendants of Asaph, were in the places prescribed by David Asaph, Heman and Jeduthun the king's seer. The gatekeepers at each did not need to leave their posts because their fellow levites made the preparations for them.

Amos 7:12

> Then Amaziah said to Amos, "Get out, you seer! go back to the land of Judah. Earn your bread there and do your prophesying there.

CHAPTER ELEVEN

THE OFFICE OF THE PROPHET

I Samuel 9:10; II Samuel 12:24; I Kings 1:38; I Kings 12:21; I Kings 17:1

1. The office of the prophet is a governmental function.

2. The prophetic office is ordained of god. Ephesians 4:11

3. Prophets are foundation ministries. Ephesians 2:20

4. Not everyone who prophesies stands in the office of a prophet. I Corinthians 12:29; I Samuel 10:9-13

5. Prophets were known as seers. Numbers 12:6, Hosea 12:10

6. Prophets operate in the ministry of helps. Ezra 5:1-2

7. A Prophet helps in perfecting saints.

8. A Prophet's ministry must be judged by another prophet or local leadership. I Corinthians 14:28-29

9. the spirit of th prophets ar subject to the prophets. I Corinthians 16:31-33

10. Every Prophet is a seer, every seer is not a Prophet.

11. The Prophet declares, the seer receives and declares only in the ear of the Prophet.

12. David's seer was Gad.

13. There are seers in administration, music, dance, drama, art, worship and praise.

14. The seer is an intercessor.

15. The seer sees for the church, city, state and nation.

CHAPTER TWELVE

THE PSYCHIC

1. A psychic is a perverted familiar spirit.

2. A psychic is the spirit of witchcraft.

3. A psychic is a thief.

4. A psychic is a trained liar.

5. A psychic speaks the will of Satan.

6. A prophet speaks the will of God

7. A prophet brings the visitation of God.

8. A psychic brings the visitation or error.

9. A psychic speaks death.

10. A prophet speaks life.

11. A psychic is the mouthpiece of Satan.

12. A prophet is the mouthpiece of God.

13. Psychics are vultures who like to prey on the lives of individuals who have been broken, bruised ad vulnerable for a lie.

14. Prophets are gatekeepers to churches, cities, states and nations. Prophets are anointed to overthrow the plans of Jezebel.

15. What does the Word "psychic" mean?

16. The psychic causes you to become an addict.

17. The psychic works witchcraft.

18. Saul's transgression was that he consulted the witch of Endor.

19. The psychic brings the curse! the curse cometh not without cause.

DAVIDIC PROPHETIC WORSHIP
STUDY QUESTIONS

Rev 12:17, And the dragon was wroth with the woman, and went to make war with the remnant of her seed, which keep the commandments of God, and have the testimony of Jesus Christ.

We BRUISE THE SERPENTS HEAD and destroy his ability to hinder the revelation to the church to bring her into the FULLNESS OF POWER, DIVINE ORDER thru the KNOWLEDGE OF WHO WE ARE...my people are destroyed, In a stupor, paralyzed and limited due to the revelation of CHRIST. We cannot move in realms of the spirit where there is no revelation.

1. Where does the government of the church receive the Pattern of worship and praise for JESUS CHRIST'S CHURCH?

2. Describe the SPIRIT OF DAVID, contrast from the SPIRIT OF MICHAEL.

3. Should there be DANCE in the church?

4. Sing a NEW SONG, what does this mean?

5. Where did DAVID run to in I Sam 19:18?

6. I Sam. 16:16-18 tells us what qualifications singers, dancers and minstrels should have?

7. Are those who bring worship appointed, or do they just join?

8. Why is it important for the SET-MAN to get involved with the worship teams, and why is it of uttermost importance that the prophet, psalmist and minstrel be married to each other?

9. What is the difference between a musician and a minstrel?

10. Corporate prophecy. Person prophecy when is it appropriate that it FLOW?

11. Elijah anointing will take the church from GILGAL TO BETHEL TO JERICHO TO JORDAN?

12. WHO STARTED THE SCHOOL OF THE PROPHETS? See I Sam 19:18, II Kings 2:-15. In the old testament there were 5 places of training for the school of the prophets. (Ramah, Gilgal, Bethel, Jericho and Jordan) what about the company of prophets?

13. Those who prophesy in the house of GOD need to be under the a........................, of another prophet.

14. The realms of Prophecy are the Prophet, the Spirit of P.........., the Gift of Prophecy, Corporate Prophecy, Pers.............. Prophecy, and the Manifestation of Prophecy. (Ephesians 4, I Cor 12, Rom 14)

15. Jeremiah said I was.............................. to be a .... Jeremiah 1:4-8.

16. The Prophetic is the mind of Christ migrating to the mind of man, let there be light, and God Prophesy...Prophets Prophesy until something happens. P.U.S.H.

1.   *Jesus giving testimony and praise through one of the saints by prophetic utterance or song of he Lore. (Heb. 2; Rev. 19:10)*

2.   *One of the manifestations of the Holy Spirit called the gift of prophecy which brings edification, exhortation and comfort to the Body of Christ (I Cor. 12:10; Rom. 12:6)*

3.   *The prophet speaking by divine utterance the mind and counsels of God and giving a rhema word for edification, direction, correction, confirmation, and instruction in righteousness. (I Cor. 14:29; II Tim. 3:16, 17).*

Prophetic Presbytery

Prophetic presbytery is when two or more prophets and/or prophetic ministers hands on and prophesy over individuals at a specified time and place. Prophetic presbyteries are conducted for several reasons:

1.   *For revealing a church member's membership ministry in the Body of Christ.*

2. *For ministering a prophetic rhema word of God to individuals.*

3. *For the revelation, clarification and confirmation of leadership ministry in the local church.*

4. *For the "laying on of hands and prophecy" over those called and properly prepared to be a five-fold minister.*

Prophetic Praying

Basically it is Spirit-directed praying. Praying with natural under-standing is asking God's help about matters of which we have natural knowledge. Prophetic praying is prophesying with prayer phraseology. It is praying out of one's spirit in his natural known tongue, flowing the same as one praying out of his spirit in unknown tongue. The prayer is on target and touches specific areas unknown in the natural to the one word of wisdom, etc. Intercessory prayer is much more effective when it moves into the realm of prophetic praying. In ministering to people in churches who do not understand or promote prophesying, prophetic min-istry can still bless the people through prophetic praying. Instead of prophesying, "thus saith the Lord" or the Lord shows me that...." you verbalize by saying, "Lord we pray for this"....Jesus, you see what he, she have been going through regarding..... or how difficult it has been in the area of..... Or overcoming.....etc.

Prophetic Counseling

Prophetic counseling serves a little different purpose than the ministry of the prophet, prophetic presbytery or general counseling. It is one-on-one ministry to help people with scriptural wisdom and insight, but also with the gifts of the Holy Spirit to discover root problems and minister deliverance, inner healing, etc. The word of knowledge and discerning of spirits are two key gifts necessary to move in this realm effectively. It allows the counselor to cut through hours of discussion and look beyond the veil of human reasoning to get right to the heart of the matter and bring resolution. This is what makes biblical counseling much more effective than the psychologist and psychiatrist who uses only human wisdom and psychology.

PROPHETHOOD

"Hood" is a covering for the head and neck and sometimes the face.
"Hood" is a state; condition; quality; character (boyhood).
"Hood" is an individual sharing a (specified) state or character (brotherhood).

1. The Prophet is the voice of God to the earth to bring men into redemption.

2. The testimony of Jesus is the Spirit of Prophecy.
   Rev. 19:10 And I fell at his feet to worship him, and he said unto me, See thou do it not: I am thy fellowservant, and of thy brethren that have the testimony of Jesus: worship God: for the testimony of Jesus is the spirit of prophecy. (KJV)

3. This testimony will bring persecution that is ordained for those who carry this witness.
   Rev 1:9 I John, who also am your brother, and companion in tribulation, and in the kingdom and patience of Jesus Christ, was in the isle that is called Patmos, for the word of God, and for the testimony of Jesus christ. (KJV)

4. You will overcome if you hold fast to your testimony, for the Word is a sword.
   Rev. 12:11 And they overcame him by the blood of the Lamb, and by the word of their testimony; and they loved not their lives unto the death. (KJV)

5. The dragon will seek you out to make war because of the testimony that exists in you and because of your inherent ability to reproduce it within your seed.
   Rev. 12:17 And the dragon was wroth with the woman, and went to make war with the remnant of her seed, which keep the commandments of God, and have the testimony of Jesus Christ (KJV)

6. Prophethood is a work that is governmental.

7. Prophethood is a work that will demand you to bring change to the environment to which you are assigned.

8. Prophethood has a responsibility to bing redemptive thinking to the people to which they are assigned.

9. Prophethood is demonstrated in the Scripture through the School of the Prophets.

10. The prophets have someone instructing and leading them.
   I Sam. 19:20 And Saul sent messengers to take David: and when they saw the company of the prophets prophesying, and Samuel standing as appointed over them, the Spirit of God was upon the messengers of Saul, and they also Prophesied. (KJV)

SPECIAL EDITION TO PROPHETIC WORSHIP
DAVIDIC PROPHETIC WORSHIP

I was taken into a vision of the Lord and began to see Dancers in the temple dancing before the Lord, with beautiful garments of white and purple, then children appeared with banners of the Lord, inscriptions of 'THE LION OF THE tribe OF JUDAH, others with 'CROWNING KING, many more appeared, then sounds of trumpets blasts, sounds of various instruments, men and women were dancing before the Lord, O, such glory, then a company of people who were sitting, stood and began to dance also before their KING, many had crowns upon their heads, they began to throw their crowns before the KING, then there appeared ANGELS descending upon the worship from the 4 corners of the earth, the worship was taken to a height that consumed my entire being, the heavens above me opened and I heard a voice saying, this is the coming glory, fresh glory that is descending upon the earth, the father has heard your cry, now he is sending down a fresh glory and you will begin to experience a new and fresh ANOINTING upon your worship, now is the time to prepare, remove the old songs, I am about to do a new thing in you, I am now placing a new song in your mouth... a song that will destroy yokes, a song that will defy the very gates of hell, a song that will t ear down strongholds in your midst and cause all your enemies to become your FOOTSTOOL, prepare for my coming...I am coming in a new and fresh way, in a way you have not even dreamed of, I Am coming as the great I Am...now worship me and I will fulfill your dreams, I will open up my treasures of riches, worship me and I will pour fresh hot lava of my love into you, I will fill the dry places in your heart, Worship Me....I will cause oceans to appear in the desert places.

WORSHIP,
DANCE,
PAGEANTRY,
MINSTRELS,
SINGERS,
PSALMIST
AND THE PROPHETS
WILL USHER IN THE
NEXT MIGHTY MOVE OF
GOD!! **THE**
APOSTOLIC
MOVEMENT

DIVINE PATTERN OF WORSHIP & PRAISE

I Chronicles 15:25, So David and the Elders of Israel, and the captains over thousands, went to bring up the Ark of the COVENANT of the Lord, out of the house of Obededom with JOY! And it came to pass, when God helped the Levites that bore the ark of the covenant of the Lord that they offered seven bullocks and seven rams. And David was clothed with a robe of linen, and all the Levites that bore the ark, and the <u>SINGERS</u> and Chenaniah the <u>Master of the SONG</u> with the <u>SINGERS</u>: David also had upon him an ephod of linen. Thus all Israel brought up the ark of the covenant of the Lord with SHOUTING, and with Sounds of CORNETS, and with TRUMPETS and with CYMBALS, making a noise with PSALTERIES and HARPS. And it came to pass, as the ark of the covenant of the Lord came to the city of David, that Michal the daughter of Saul looking out at the window saw King David DANCING and PLAYING: and she despised him in her heart.

Chapter 15:2, Then David said, none ought to carry the ARK but the Levites: for them hath the Lord chosen to carry the ARK of the God, and to minister unto him forever.

And David was afraid of God that day saying, How can I bring the ARK of the GOD home to me?

And David spake to the CHIEF of the Levites to APPOINT their brethren to be SINGERS with instruments of MUSIC, PSALTERIES, and the HARP and CYMBALS, SOUNDING, by lifting up the voice with joy!

And it came to pass when the priest were come out of the holy place, also the Levites which were of the singers, all of them ASAPH, of HEMAN, of JEDUTHUN, with their brethren, being arrayed in white linen, having cymbals and psalteries and harps, stood at the east end of the altar, and with them were a hundred and twenty priests sounding with trumpets, and it came to pass as the trumpeters and the singers were as one, to make one sound to be heard in praising and thanking the Lord, and when they had lifted up their voice with the trumpets and cymbals and instruments of music, and praised the Lord saying FOR HE IS GOOD, FOR HIS MERCY ENDURED FOREVER, THAT THE HOUSE WAS FILLED WITH A CLOUD, EVEN THE PRIEST COULD NOT STAND TO MINISTER BY REASON OF THE GLORY CLOUD. For the glory of the Lord had filled the house of God.

GLORY, What exactly is GLORY? Glory is the tangible evidences of GOD MANIFESTED POWER AND RIGHTEOUSNESS IN YOUR LIFE, appearing as wealth, health, blessings, strength, breakthrough in your life abundantly and every yoke of SATAN destroyed. GLORY is not just a choir making noise, ISRAEL was defeated by the Philistines because the ark was stolen. The ARK was symbolic of GOD'S ANOINTING AND GLORY, NOT JUST GOD'S PRESENCE, many a musician can create God's presence, but only GOD SENT MINSTRELS can create GLORY! It's time to bring the ARK back to its rightful place, the church, it's time to bring the DANCERS back to the church, it's time to bring the SONG OF THE LORD back to the TEMPLE.

ORDER OF MINSTRELS, SINGERS AND MUSICIANS IN THE HOUSE OF GOD

David the mighty PSALMIST of ISRAEL was given the divine pattern of worship, singers, dancers and minstrels.

ANOINTED MINSTRELS are rare to find, they have an ear and an eye for the sound of GOD in the earth in present truth of this time. Minstrels play under the anointing, they bring fresh glory from heavens kitchen, they don't copy from the secular world and try to pervert the temple. The musicians must live at the altar and get the mind of Christ for worship in the house.

The singers and musicians were appointed, separated, instructed, directed, had rank, and were skillful. The minstrel, psalmist and prophet are in an office in the church, five fold ministry gift. Minstrels are not in the entertainment business, they are creating GLORY! True minstrels are in agreement with the set man and work under leadership. True minstrels ministry is solely toward the heavenlies sphere and not directed toward themselves as becoming celebrities, they are a worship unto GOD! True minstrels are INTERCESSORS. They set the climate, the atmosphere of the worship. Worship will take on a fresh dimension of GOD in our services, spontaneous worship without practice, new song given during worship, a song coming directly from the throne, the key is the release of true INTERCESSORS IN THE HOUSE OF GOD, AND CHURCH LEADERSHIP NOT AFRAID TO LET GO OF THE OLD TO COME INTO THE NEW. FRESH OIL IS NOW BEING POURED FROM THE HEAVENLIES, did not GOD say I will pour out of my spirit upon all flesh! We were ordained to give GOD glory, to be the very glory of the father in the earth, he commands us to give him praise and worship...

As Elijah prayed, GO GET ME A MINSTREL!!!! MINSTRELS ARISE... open up the heavenlies, shut down the negative vibes of the adversary from interfering with that which the father has ordained for particular service.

PSALMS 68:25 The singers went before the players on the instruments followed after, among them were the DAMSELS playing with TIMBRELS.

PAGEANTRY AND DANCE

PAGEANTRY expresses the GREATNESS of the father, it expresses the beauty of the father, the brightness of his glory in the earth. We cannot conceive with the natural eye the magnificent glory of God but thru dance and pageantry we can display our love and adoration to God, expressing it with all our might and strength in the dance and in pageantry. The church needs a fresh revelation on displaying God's glory in the earth in theater, drama, the arts and pageantry. The 21st century church will take on a entire new look, the gifts of drama, arts, and dance will return to the temple. Churches will need to build their stages for drama, dance and theater. The gospel will be dramatized.

When an assembly or congregation worships with a liberal display of flags, dance, prophetic gestures, banners, singing, mime, we will see a GLORIOUS DISPLAY WITHOUT SHAME OF GOD'S KINGS AND PRIESTS IN THE EARTH. For too long the church as been ashamed to dance with dignity together before their GOD, but the world dances before their god. The Priests are to lead out in the dance. The devil hates the church when the entire congregation SHABACK, and HALAL and RAVE before the TRUE KING. Satan's role has been to steal the glory, to pervert music and bring glory to himself, that's why Lucifer was kicked out of heaven with 1/3 of the other angels who crossed over to pervert the true to false worship. THE SPIRIT OF MICHAEL tries to invade the church causing believers to be afraid to express their true love to the Father, yet many were redeemed from the dance juke joint world. In the satanic court unbelievers dance with such might to a fallen angel all night, how much more shall we the body of Christ dance HILARIOUSLY before the KING OF GLORY.

IT'S TIME TO WORSHIP AND DANCE BEFORE OUR GOD IN THE SPIRIT AND IN TRUTH. May the SPIRIT OF DAVID COME UPON YOU.......

(please send your testimonies of how your have been blessed by this manual, see address on back).

DEFINITIONS

PROPHET: nay or nab (gnaw-bee) an inspired man, a spokesman, a man who has been assigned by the Holy Spirit to speak on behalf of God and placed in the earth to bring men into redemption. (Ex 4:10, Jer. 1:3, Acts 2:22)

PROPHETESS: nebiv'ah (neb-ee-yew') is a female prophet. In the Old Testament she was a prophet's wife. By implication, also a poetess (Judges 4:45, Ex 15:20, II Kings 22:14, Isa 8:3)

PROPHETHOOD: The state of combination of serving in the office of the Prophet; the brotherhood of Prophets and Prophetess.

PROPHETIC GIFTS: The four levels of prophecy, which include the manifestation of Prophecy, the grace gift of Prophecy, the spirit of Prophecy and the office of the Prophet.

PSYCHIC: A person positioned by Satan to aid principalities and powers of darkness. A person who illegally enters the supernatural to obtain information.

SEER: ro'eh, to see, literally or figuratively. Providere (Latin), to see beforehand. It is the old testament term for "Prophet" and emphasized the means by which revelation was perceived. (I Sam. 9-9, I Chron. 29:29)

SERVANT: ebed (eh'-bed), a bondsman; abad (aw-bad), to work, serve, enslave, worshipper.

SCHOOL OF THE PROPHETS: naioth (school), a dwelling place or lodging. It is a haven, place of rest for Prophets. Five places of training included: Ramah, Bethel, Gilgal, Jericho and Jordan.

VISION: Chazah, to gaze at; mentally to perceive, behold, look at. The term also refers to a person's personal sight (viewing) of the Divine Presence of the Lord. (I Sam. 19:20, 2 Kings 2:3-5)

BIBLICAL REFERENCE

Amos 3:7	Isaiah 3:2
Ephesians 3:3-5	Ezekiel 2:5; 33:33
Ephesians 2:19-20	Hosea 9:7
Revelation 18:20; 22:9	Zechariah 1:5
II Chronicles 20:20	Matthew 7:15; 10:41; 13:57
Ephesians 4:11-13	Luke 4:24; 11:47; 24:19
Mark 1:2-3, 6:4	John 4:44, 23:29
Acts 3:20-21; & 37	Luke 1:76; 7:16, 28, 39, 13:33
Jeremiah 1:29; 26; 37:19	John 4:19; 7:40, 52
I Corinthians 12:28-29; 14:37	Acts 26:27
Numbers 11:29	I Peter 1:10
Exodus 7:1; 12:6	
Deut. 13:1; 18:15; 34:10	
I Samuel 10:12; 19:24	
I Kings 13:11; 18:22; 22:7	
II Kings 3:11; 5:8	
I Chronicles 16:22	
Psalms 105:15; 74:9	

In closing, as the Church, the Bride of Christ prepares for the coming of our crowning King, our business must be soul winning, ushering others into the Kingdom.

Avoid extremes in truths or excesses, even with the move of the Prophetic and Apostolic. Stay balanced. Avoid error. Preach Jesus Christ and win your city. Establish the Church in present truth. The Glory cloud has moved. The trumpet has blasted. It is time to go on into perfection.

EXPLANATION AND DEFINITIONS
OF
PRESENT TRUTH PROPHETIC T ERMS

In the Old Testament, the School of the prophets had five places of training: Ramah, Bethel, Gilgal, Jericho, and Jordan. Among those who directed such schools were Samuel, Elijah and Elisha. I Samuel 19:18 speaks of Samuel's involvement in the School of the Prophets at Ramah. Many believe that it was here that David was trained and taught how to worship God.

So David fled, and escaped and came to Samuel to Ramah, and told him all that Saul had done to him. And he and Samuel went and dwelt in Naioth.

Elijah's involvement in the School of the Prophets is revealed in II Kings 2:9

And it came to pass, when they were gone over, that Elijah said unto Elisha, Ask what I shall do for thee, before I be taken away from thee. And Elisha said, I pray thee, let a double portion of thy spirit be upon me.

FIVE-FOLD MINISTRY:

These are the five-fold ascension gift ministers as revealed in Eph. 4:11 — Apostle, Evangelist, Pastor and Teacher. they are not gifts of the Holy Spirit per se, but an extension of Christ's headship ministry to the Church. Their primary ministry and function is to teach, train, activate and mature the saints for the work of their ministries.

Apostle:

One of the five-fold ministries of Eph. 4:11, The Apostle is a founda-tion laying ministry (Eph. 2:20) which is seen in the N.T. establishing new churches (Paul's missionary Journeys), correcting error by establish-ing proper order and structure (First Epistle to the Corinthians), an acting as an oversight ministry which fathers other ministries (I Cor. 4:15, II Cor. 4:28). The N.T. Apostle has a revelatory anointing (Eph. 3:5), and frequently demonstrates signs, wonders and miracles. More will be known and manifested concerning the apostle during the next restorational movement.

Prophet

*A man of God whom Christ has given the ascension gift of a "prophet."
(Eph. 4:11, I Cor. 12:28, I Cor. 14:29, Acts: 29; Acts 11:27; Acts
13:1). A prophet is one of the five-fold ascension gift ministers who are
an extension of Christ's ministry to the Church. An anointed minister
who has the gifted ability to perceive and speak the specific mind of
Christ to individuals, churches, businesses and nations. GREEK:
"prophetes" (prof-ay-tace) a foreteller, an inspired speaker. (STRONG'S
Concordance, Pg 62; VINES' Concordance Pg. 894) A proclaimer of a
divine message, denoted among Greeks as an interpreter of the oracles of
gods. In the Septuagint it is the translation of the word "roeh" — a seer
— indicating that the prophet was one who had immediate intercourse
with God (I Sam 9:9). It also translates the word "Nabhi," meaning
either "one in whom the message from God springs forth, or one to
whom anything is secretly communicated." (Amos 3:7; Eph. 3:5)*

Prophetess GREEK:

*"prophetis"— the feminine of prophet (Gr. Prophetess). A woman of God
who has been given the divine prophetic ability to perceive and speak
the mind of Christ on specific matters to particular people. STRONGS:
a "female foreteller or an inspired woman." A specially called woman
who functions like the New Testament prophet to minister to the Body
of Christ with inspired speaking and prophetic utterance (Acts 2:17;
21:9; Luke 2:36; Is. 8:3; II Chron. 34:22; Jude 4:4; Ex. 15:20).
Prophetess is the proper title for a woman with this ascension gifts and
calling. Prophet is the proper title for a man with this ascension gift
and calling.*

Evangelist

*The traditional view of the evangelist is a bearer of the "Good News",
proclaiming the gospel to the unbelieving world. This is exemplified by
modern day evangelists who preach the message of salvation in crusades
and the like. However, Phillip, the N.T. Evangelist mentioned in Acts
21:8 demonstrated a strong super-natural dimension to the
Evangelistic ministry. Phillip preached the gospel to the lost (Acts 8:5)
moved in miracles (8:26), had revelation knowledge (8:29), and was
super-naturally translated from Gaza to Azotus (8:26,40). We are
looking forward to the restoration of this type of Prophetic Evangelist to
the Body of Christ.*

Pastor

"Poiment", "a shepherd, on who tends herds or flocks (not merely one who feeds them), is used metaphorically of Christian pastors. "Episkopeo" (overseer, bishop) is an overseer, and "Pesbuteros (elder) is another term for the same person as bishop or overseer. (Vines). The title normally given to the senior minister of the local church, regardless of his five-fold calling. A shepherding ministry to feed and care for the flock. Responsibilities that appear connected with pastoral ministry include oversight and care of the saints, providing spiritual food for their growth and development leadership, guidance and counsel. Prophetic pastors not only do the things normally associated with pasturing, but also move in supernatural graces and gifting of God (prophesying, word of knowledge, healing) and have the vision and willingness to develop the saints in their gifts and callings.

Teacher

An instructor of truth (II Tim. 3:16) A scripture is given by inspiration of God, and is profitable for doctrine, for reproof, for correction, for instruction in righteousness. New Testament Prophetic Teacher is one who not only teaches the letter of the word, but ministers with divine life and Holy Spirit anointing (II Cor. 3:6). He exhibits keen spiritual insight and discernment into the Word of God and its personal application to believers.

Prophetic Ministers

Prophetic ministers are all other ministers who do not have the office of the "prophet" but who do hold another office of the five-fold ministry and believe that there are prophets in the Church today. They may move in prophetic ministry by prophesying with the gift of prophecy, or by giving personal prophecy with a prophetic presbytery, do prophetic counseling and ministry with gifts of the Holy Spirit, or minister in prophetic worship. All five-fold New Testament ministers in whichever office should be able to speak a rhema word revealing the mind and purpose of God for specific situations and people (II Cor. 3:6; I Cor. 14:31).

Prophetic Anointing and Mantle

An in-depth study of the word "anoint" reveals that it was used to consecrate people to a particular position or ministry. In ministering with prophetic anointing, it means you are enduring people with the presence of Christ and the gifts and graces of the Holy Spirit. Isa. 10:27 declare yokes are destroyed because of the anointing. In present day application this means the manifested presence of God to meet specific needs.

To say a person has a prophetic anointing means that they have the calling to move in the prophetic ministry. It does not necessarily mean this person has the calling of the office of "prophet". Prophetic mantel has a similar meaning. If someone has prophesied you have a prophetic mantle, it implies that you have the gifted ability to minister in prophetic ministry, to what received will be determined by time and use (Ex. 28:41; Psalms 2:2; 23; 105:15; Zec. 4:6; Heb. 1:19).

Prophecy

GREEK: "propheteia", a noun which "signifies the speaking forth of the mind and counsel of God. It is the declaration of which cannot be known by natural means. It is the forth-telling of the will of God, whether with reference to the past, the present, and the future" (VINES, pg.8893). New Testament prophecy functions in three realms:

Logos

GREEK: "word" — the unchanging, inerrant, creative and inspired word of God (See Ps. 119:89 "Forever, O Lord, thy word (logos) is settled in heaven.") (See also II Tim 3:26; I Cor. 2:13) Logos is the entire written Word of God — the Bible. It is the complete revelation of God — His personage, character, plan and eternal purpose as found in the Scripture.

Rhema

GREEK: "word" — derived from the verb "to speak". (See Rom. 10 "Faith cometh by hearing and hearing by the word (rhema) of God.") A rhema is a word or an illustration God speaks directly to it and us addresses our personal, particular situation. It is a timely, Holy Spirit-inspired Word from the logos that brings life, power and faith to perform and fulfill it. Its significance is exemplified in the injunction to take the "sword of the Spirit, which is the word (rhema) of God (Eph. 6:17). It can be reached through others such as by a prophetic word, or be an illumination given to one directly in their personal meditation time in the bible or in prayer.

The logos is the fixed word of God — the Scriptures — and the rhema is a particular portion in line with the logos brought forth by the Spirit to be applied directly to something in our personal experience.

Prophetic Warfare Praise and Worship

They are biblical expressions of praise and adoration (singing, clapping, dancing, lifting of hands, bowing, etc.) that are directed to God, inspired and directed by the Holy Spirit, and which comes forth from the heart of man. Prophetic worship is where God's voice is heard and His presence felt as Christ begins to sing an express praise to the Father through His people. (Heb. 2:1; Ps. 22:22; Rev 19:10). These high praises of God both exalt the Lord and accomplish spiritual warfare in the heavenliness (Ps. 14:6-9; Eph. 6:12; II Cor. 10:4-6). It is worship that is expressed obedience to a prompting of God that brings forth a prophetic word; mantle or anointing that results in the manifestation of God's power (II Cor. 20:14-22; II Kings 3:15; I Sam. 10:5,6).

Prophetic Song

A song that is inspired, anointed and directed by the Holy Spirit through an individual; usually spontaneous in nature, which expresses the mind of God in musical form. It is literally prophecy through song (referred to in the New Testament as spiritual songs) (See Col 3:16; Eph. 5:19). These songs are directed to man for the purpose of edification, exhortation and comfort or may be directed to God as the Holy Spirit helps us express our deep devotion, that we could not ordinarily express by ourselves (Heb. 2:12; Rom. 8:27; Eph. 3:17 — "The Lord their God....will joy over you or through you with singings.")

Prophetic Praise — Dance and Sign

Physical movements that are inspirational and anointed by the Holy Spirit and many times accompanied by prophetic song (song of the Lord; spiritual songs) (See Ex. 15:20-21; I Sam. 21:11). It is used in praise; adoration and worship to God, which can in itself bring in the prophetic mantle (I 18:6). It may be spontaneous or choreographed (preplanned). At times, it may communicate divine thoughts, ideas and purpose — a visible expression of what God is saying (Acts 21:10; Job 42:5— "My ears have heard you, but now my eyes have seen you!").

DEFINITIONS

PROPHET: nay or nab (gnaw-bee) an inspired man, a spokesman, a man who has been assigned by the Holy Spirit to speak on behalf of God and placed in the earth to bring men into redemption. (Ex 4:10, Jer. 1:3, Acts 2:22)

PROPHETESS: nebiv'ah (neb-ee-yew') is a female prophet. In the Old Testament she was a prophet's wife. By implication, also a poetess (judges 4:45, Ex 15:20, II Kings 22:14, Isa 8:3)

PROPHETHOOD: The state of combination of serving in the office of the Prophet; the brotherhood of Prophets and Prophetess.

PROPHETIC GIFTS: The four levels of prophecy, which include the manifestation of Prophecy, the grace gift of Prophecy, the spirit of Prophecy and the office of the Prophet.

PSYCHIC: A person positioned by Satan to aid principalities and powers of darkness. A person who illegally enters the supernatural to obtain information.

SEER: ro'eh, to see, literally or figuratively. Providere (Latin), to see beforehand. It is the old testament term for "Prophet" and emphasized the means by which revelation was perceived. (I Sam 9-9, I Chron 29:29)

SERVANT: ebed (eh'-bed), a bondsman; abad (aw-bad), to work, serve, enslave, worshipper.

SCHOOL OF THE PROPHETS: naioth (school), a dwelling place or lodging. It is a haven, place of rest for Prophets. Five places of training included: Ramah, Bethel, Gilgal, Jericho and Jordan.

VISION: Chazah, to gaze at; mentally to perceive, behold, look at. The term also refers to a person's personal sight (viewing) of the Divine Presence of the Lord. (I Sam 19:20, 2 Kings 2:3-5)

Let the Prophets Speak Congress Coming
In every Major City in America

Call today become a Sponsor in your City, Activate the Prophetic Congress in your Church and City,

Prophet Israel & Gerri will conduct the

"School of the Apostles/Prophets" Congress including Teaching Manual for all your leaders, day sessions for your City, Night Services Prophetic Breakthru Apostolic Preaching!!!

Contact us at 206.898.8685, email at Kingdomdominion1@earthlink.net

About the Author ....

Prophet Israel & Gerri are Founders and CEO's of the <u>DREAM-CITY Northwest Gatekeeper's and Kingdom Dominion Embassy Church.</u> Prophet Israel leaves an indelible mark upon each life, with his Apostolic preaching, anointed skillful prophetic wisdom insights, accuracy in presenting present day truth to the Body of Christ, he sits on the cutting edge of creating a true 3rd Millennium Powerbase church training Diplomatic Ambassadors impacting the Pacific Northwest Region and taking NATIONS!

The Breakthrough-Vision is creating economic synergy and committed to the task of strategically positioning businesses, developing non-profit organizations, churches, individuals and the community in directing the <u>TRANSFER AND DELIVERY OF WEALTH to stagnated and morally degenerated inner cities of America. Dream city Northwest Gatekeeper's and Kingdom Dominion embassy</u> purpose to ignite the entrepreneurial enterprise spirit, implementation of providing businesses and churches with the tools to become self-sufficient through the organization of <u>COMMUNITY CREDIT UNIONS</u>, grocery stores, newspapers, business plazas, housing for the poor, vision to ultimately create an incorporate City to create a new economy generating generational wealth.

<u>In October 2005 Seattle Empowerment Wealth Business Summits was launched by DREAMCITY Northwest Gatekeeper's (501C3) and Kingdom Dominion Wisdom Centre purpose to establish Economic Capital Creating "Seattle Wall Street" a marketplace building wealth to IMPACT NATIONS, thru Home Ownership programs, business Training, banking Center, a Team of Community Leaders Monthly Meet to collaborate and create wealth and eradicate poverty in our inner cities, destroy the slave–wage mentality, thereby impacting our city economic forecast. Summits are held throughout the city of Seattle Empowering people to become self reliant, creation of a RESOURCE CENTER TO PROVIDE ASSISTANCE IN FULFILLING DREAMS.</u>

Dr. Barsh started his first church in 1980, at the age of 22 while a student at Washington State University, was ordained in 1994 in the office of Prophet by the Presbytery of Revival International Church from Portland, Oregon, under the ministry of Apostle Roper. Dr. Barsh for over 9 years pastored Northwest Christian Embassy, where he started a full k-12 grade Academy, and Childcare Center in Tacoma, Washington. He conducted the West Coast Prophets Congress each year, is in demand as a Conference speaker across America. Now has 4 books being published. *"Millionaire Status", "The School of the Prophets" and "Uncovering the conspiracy against the Prophetic Anointing" a 31 day Prophetic Affirmation for Wealth Creation, a manual designed to training church leader to expand their Vision to take Cities.* Dr. Barsh is a LaGrange High School Graduate 1977, received his bachelor's of Arts degree from Washington State University 1989, received a Doctorate of Divinity degree from the prestige Bishop Hardy's Theological Seminary in 1992, was a USA Army Commission Officer 1st Lieutenant in the Personnel Manager, for over 10 years, and in 1994 received a Letter of Recognition for his outstanding Community Services from the Mayor of Puyallup Washington.

THE UNIVERSITY SCHOOL OF THE APOSTLES/ PROPHETS CERTIFICATION QUESTIONS

CHAPTER I

Part 1. Please fill in the blanks with the appropriate answers.

1. Elisha's request of his mentor, Elijah, before his departing this world was, "Let a _____ of thy spirit be upon me." (2 Kings 2:9)

2. You cannot work effectively in the vision of the land unless you have the _____ of the leader.

3. Elisha called Elijah _____   _____ (2Kings 2:12).

4. The reason the students in the School of the Prophets were called "sons of the prophets" was not that their fathers were prophets, but because they were students of _____ _____ and _____. Their instructors were _____.

5. To be a "son of the prophet," you had to have the attitude of a _____.

6. A prophet operates within the _____ ministry.

7. According to 2 Kings 3:11, one of Elisha's tasks as a servant to Elijah was to _____.

8. God does not make leaders. He makes _____ and _____ then become leaders.

9. If you are called to minister, then you are called to _____.

10. New Testament leaders were trained primarily by " _____   _____" experience.

11. In ministry, the attitude of service allows more to be learned by _____ and _____ than by being filled with information.

12. To be a true leader, you must have a _____ heart.

13. A true prophet of God will help _____ the house of the Lord, while a false prophet will try to _____ it.

PART 2. Please put a T in the blank if the statement is True; F if the statement is False. If the statement is False, please indicate why.

_____ 1. Samuel was an instructor in the School of the Prophets.

_____ 2. Elijah was an instructor in the School of the Prophets.

_____ _3. Elisha asked Elijah for a double portion of the Holy Spirit.

CHAPTER II

Part 1. Please fill in the blanks with the appropriate answers.

1. Elijah was a _____
_____ to Elisha.

2. God is a God of _____. He is called "the God of _____, _____, and _____.

3. It is believed that before Abram moved into covenant with God, his home was most likely a _____.

4. Sarai means "_____ _____." She was responsible for the idea that Abram should give her children through her maid, Hagar.

5. After Hagar conceived, she was _____ in Sarai's eyes (Genesis 16:4)

6. When God made covenant with Abram, his name was changed to _____.

CHAPTER III

Part 1. Please fill in the blanks with the appropriate answers.

1. In a company of prophets, you will find _____,
_____, and _____.

2. Students in the School of the Prophets were potential spiritual
leaders in Israel who would speak for the _____ of
God _____ the word of the Lord.

3. When Saul's messengers who were sent to take
David came into the company of prophets, they also
_____. (1 Samuel 19:20)

4. In 1 Samuel 19:20, we see that Samuel was
_____ over the prophets.

5. As their appointed leader, Samuel brought
_____, _____, and
_____, to keep them in the divine flow.

6. God is a God of _____.

7. Saul and Barnabas could not go forth in ministry until they were
_____ by the church.

8. Many people want to enter the ministry, but they don't want to
wait until the _____ _____ _____.

9. You can only overcome evil with _____. David never
spoke _____ concerning Saul.

10. Saul's messengers began to see _____ perspective
instead of Saul's.

11. Man can move in _____ power rather than in the
power of the Holy Spirit.

12. The Holy Spirit will give you the heavenly Father's
_____ in prayer.

13. To prophesy with the motive to show how spiritual you are is
to _____ the gift of God.

14. Every prophet (or believer) must be watchful, mindful, and function under _____.

15. It is crucial that we allow the Spirit of God to lead us in the _____ from on High.

Part 2. Please put a T in the blank if the statement is True, F if the statement is False.

_____ 1. In the School of the Prophets at Ramah, Samuel was responsible for orchestrating the move of the spirit.

_____ 2. Whatever the leader is doing when you come under his covering, you will do the same thing.

_____ 3. Intercession can get into an area of witchcraft if it is not based upon the Word of God.

CHAPTER IV

Part 1. Please fill in the blanks with the appropriate answers.

1. The only difference the occult and the church is that one is _____ Christ while the other is _____ of Christ.

2. When people lay hands on you, their _____ is transferred to you.

3. When Moses had so much responsibility he couldn't handle it himself, the Lord transferred Moses' _____ to those to whom authority was delegated.

4. Moses' spirit was transferred to the seventy elders so they could "…bear the _____ of the people with thee, that thou bear it not thyself alone."

5. You should not give your spirit to someone unless you _____ him (or her).

6. The laying on of hands is for the purpose of _____ doing the _____ of the Lord.

7. There should never be a departation unless there is firs an _____.

8. When the spirit of Moses fell upon the seventy elders, "they

_____, and did not cease" (Numbers 11:25)

9. The spirit of _____ will lead you into all
_____.

10. The Spirit of truth will lead you out when the leadership is
_____.

11. In the New Testament, when the twelve apostles laid
their hands upon the seven men (Acts 6:16), it is believed,
because of the fruit that followed, that an _____
_____ was transferred to these seven men.

12. It is possible for God to turn you into another person when you
begin to _____, just as He did Saul.

Part 2. Please put a T in the blank if the statement True; F if the
statement is False. If the statement is False, please indicate why.

_____ 1. The laying on of hands denotes covenant.

_____ 2. In the laying on of hands, there is no difference
between a "left hand blessing" and a "right hand blessing."

_____ 3. Even the ungodly can speak the oracles of God.

Chapter V:

Part 1. Please fill in the blanks with the appropriate answers.

1. Bethel means "_____ _____
_____."

2. The two different orders of prophets are _____ house
prophets and _____ house of prophets.

3. There is a stench to "out house" prophets when they have not
submitted to the _____ of the local house.

4. As pastors and leaders, we are to know those who _____
among us.

5. I encourage prophets to function only in the local church or in
churches when they are in _____

6. To participate in a communion service is to participate in a
_____ meal.

7. Strong soul ties with family can hinder you from entering into
_____ with God.

8. One of the signs of a true prophet is you begin to see the
_____.

Part 2. Please put a T in the blank if the statement True; F if the
statement is False. If the statement is False, please indicate why.

_____ 1. There is a protocol in the realm of the Spirit, just as
there is a protocol in the natural.

_____ 2. Deception can overcome a true prophet of God if he
steps outside of his realm of authority.

_____ 3. A prophet can use his gift to manipulate another person
(or prophet).

_____ 4. It is not profitable to mock the anointed prophets of
God.

Chapter VI

Part 1. Please fill in the blanks with the appropriate answer.

1. Gilgal means " _____ _____."

2. Samuel's name means " _____ _____."

3. The prophets in training under Samuel were called "
_____ _____ _____ _____ " (
1 Samuel 10:5). However the prophets training under Elijah
and Elisha were known as " _____ _____ _____
_____."

4. If a person's ministry is not correct at home, the same qualities
will manifest in _____ ministry.

5. When operating under authority, God will give you
_____.

6. To become _____ of leadership will hinder your work.

7. The sons of the prophet learned how to operate in the Spirit. What are the five (5) specific areas mentioned that they also learned in the School of the Prophets?

a. _____ b. _____ c. _____
d. _____ e. _____

8. The law of use basically says, "Whatever you do not use, you _____."

9. In the School of the Prophets, the students received "_____ _____."

10. In the prophet's role to the king, they moved into the _____ arena.

11. Name the three (3) anointings that took place in David's life.

a. _____ b. _____
c. _____

12. It is possible for there to be _____ _____ in your life before you come into the full purpose of that which God has ordained and set apart for you.

Part 2. Please put a T in the blank if the statement True; F if the statement is False. If the statement is False, please indicate why.

_____ 1. You can be a great leader, yet have a poor image as a father.

_____ 2. To gather together with a body of believers in a church is different than assembling yourself with them.

Chapter VII

Part 1. Please fill in the blanks with the appropriate answers.

1. _____ was David's seer. He saw for David.

2. Please give the five (5) descriptions for seer that was listed:

a. _____ b. _____ c. _____
d. _____ e. _____

3. If you hear and obey the words of a prophet, you will
_____.

4. Judah means _____. When Saul pursued David,
Gad told David to go into the land of Judah, the place of
_____ (1 Samuel 22:5)

5. God sets _____ and _____ in the house
of the Lord to bring structure to the order of the house.

6. The prophet is set in the church to _____ the church.

7. The prophet Agabus brought _____ to Paul
ahead of time that he would be bound and delivered into the hands
of the Gentiles in Jerusalem (Acts 21).

8. Even in the Old Testament, _____ played an
important role in the prophetic ministry.

9. In 1 Chronicles 25:3, we see that Jeduthun prophesied with a
harp, giving _____ and _____ to God.

10. Heman was the King's _____.

11. Iddo was a _____ against Jeroboam, a wicked king.

12. Every believer is called to be a porter (a door or gate keeper),
for a believer is a city of God. If a believer is not a porter, the
_____ (Satan and his crew) will come in and destroy
you.

13. Gate keepers are _____ or _____.

14. The measure of your _____ to authority
will determine the degree of your authority.

15. The ministry of the seer is _____, while the
ministry of the prophet is _____ (or declaring).

16. A prophet is an inspired person who has been assigned by the _____ to speak on behalf of God.

17. There is a difference between _____ and the _____ of time.

18. In the office of prophet, you move more in a _____ mode, while the seer moves in more of a _____ mode.

19. Moses was God's _____ to Pharaoh.

20. Our ears need to be _____ so we can hear the word of the Lord.

Part 2. Please put a T in the blank if the statement True; F if the statement is False. If the statement is False, please indicate why.

_____ 1. God still wants to give seers unto leaders.

_____ 2. Prophecy can come forth on musical instruments.

_____ 3. Many intercessors and musicians move in the realm of the prophetic.

_____ 4. The seer is not necessarily a prophet.

_____ 5. God will allow you to see some things that you are never able to declare.

Chapter VIII

Part 1. Please fill in the blanks with the appropriate answers.

1. The prophet is in more of a _____ mode, sharing what he hears from on High, while the seer is in more of a _____ mode, seeing visions from on High.

2. Rebekah inquired of the Lord when she was pregnant, because the babies (twins Esau and Jacob) struggled together within her. The Lord told Rebekah, "…Two _____ are in the womb…" (Genesis 25:23). Esau and Jacob were wrestling in the womb for _____.

3. Esau means _____ _____, while Jacob means _____. Jacob's name was later changed to _____, which means "he shall rule as God."

4. When a believer understands that he is the Israel of God, he will understand that he is to _____ as God here in the earth.

5. God brings _____ to men through the vehicle of vision.

6. The word vision in Hebrew is interpreted "without a _____ _____ ." God then is really saying, "Without a vision or _____ _____ My people perish."

7. A visionary is someone who imagines how things _____ _____ and pays little regard to how they actually are.

8. The vision of the Lord will bring _____ and _____.

9. That which we see in the natural is a lie if it is not in agreement with God's _____.

Part 2. Please put a T in the blank if the statement True; F if the statement is False. If the statement is False, please indicate why.

_____ 1. You cannot hide from a seer.

_____ 2. The seer does not see with his physical eyes; he sees with the eye of his spirit and relays what he sees back to his brain.

Chapter IX

Part 1. Please fill in the blanks with the appropriate answers.

1. God wants to give us a _____ _____ and a _____ _____ (Proverbs 20:12)

2. Second Kings 6:12 says the prophet of God knew the words being spoken in the _____ of the king.

3. This is the hour God is raising up His prophets to speak the _____ of the Lord in situations to bring _____.

4. In 2 Kings 6:16, Elisha told his servant who had inquired about the forces of the enemy, "…Fear not, for they that be with us are _____ than they that be with them."

5. When Elisha asked the Lord to open the eyes of his servant to see, what did the servant see? (Verse 17) _____
_____
_____

6. The realm of the Spirit is the _____, and the realm of the natural is a _____.

7. God smote the enemy with _____ according to the word of Elisha (2 Kings 6:18). To be smitten with blindness meant they were in a place of _____
_____.

Part 2. Please put a T in the blank if the statement True; F if the statement is False. If the statement is False, please indicate why.

_____ 1. Many people are blind to the revelation of God.

Chapter X

Part 1. Please fill in the blanks with the appropriate answers.

1. Urim means _____, _____, or _____, while Thummim means _____,____
_____, _____ and _____.

2. The Urim and Thummim were used for the purpose of the _____, the nation of _____, or the well-being of the _____.

3. We can compare the Urim and Thummim to the _____ spoken of in Revelation 2:5 where Jesus said through John, "…I will come unto thee quickly, and will remove they candlestick out of his place, except thou repent."

4. The Urim and Thummim were a means of _____ and _____, just as Jesus is to believers today.

5. The Urim and Thummim were elements of judgment which helped to discern the _____ and _____ of God.

Chapter XI

Part 1. Please fill in the blanks with the appropriate answers.

1. Romans 12:1 and 2 is relevant for us today. What two (2) primary commands are given to us in these verses? a. _____
_____ b._____
_____

2. According to Romans 12:2, why are we to renew our minds? __
_____

_____
_____

3. The mind is the seat of our _____
_____.

4. Prayer changes things, but it also changes
_____.

5. Meditation means "to _____ to oneself."

6. Meditation of the Word means _____ and _____ the Word over and over.

7. The key to God's prosperity is found in Joshua 1:8. Please quote this verse:

_____

_____

_____

_____

_____

8. We are to be_____ of the Word and the _____ manifested.

Part 2. Please put a T in the blank if the statement True; F if the statement is False. If the statement is False, please indicate why.

_____ 1. You cannot know the perfect will of God if your mind is not renewed.

_____ 2. When we labor in prayer, we change God.

_____ 3. There is no such thing as a permissive will of God.

Chapter XII

Part I. Please fill in the blanks with the appropriate answers.

1. God always takes us from _____ to _____.

2. When a person makes Jesus Christ his Lord and Savior, the _____ is removed.

3. Glory means _____, _____, or _____.

4. The glory Jacob received was Laban's _____.

5. Haggai 2:9 says, "The _____ (or wealth) of this latter house shall be greater than of the former, saith the Lord of hosts...."

Part 2. Please put a T in the blank if the statement True; F if the statement is False. If the statement is False, please indicate why.

_____ 1. God can take that which is a mistake and weave it into His plan, pattern and purpose.

Chapter XIII

Part 1. Please fill in the blanks with appropriate answers.

1. Whatever you _____ you become. You become whatever you worship.

2. The _____ is hid from people when they are lost.

3. The light of the Gospel of Jesus Christ is the _____ of God (2 Corinthians 4:4).

4. It is _____ (the god of this world) who has blinded the eyes of those who believe not (Corinthians 4:4)

5. God wants to command the _____ to shine out of our darkness.

6. Your present struggles are preparing you for future
_____.

7. Please give the three (3) descriptions of the Word of God found in Hebrews 4:12:

a. _____ b._____
c._____

8. The Word of God is able to discern the _____ and _____ of a person's heart (Hebrews 4:12)

Part 2. Please put a T in the blank if the statement True; F if the statement is False. If the statement is False, please indicate why.

_____ 1. All things are open unto Jesus' eyes.

_____ 2. Some people want to know God from a distance.

_____ 3. It is just as important to hear the words someone is not saying as it is to hear the words they are saying.

Chapter XIV

Part 1. Please fill in the blanks with the appropriate answers.

1. Gad, David's seer, brought a heavy message to David in 1 Chronicles 21:11 and 12, because of David's disobedience. What were the three choices God gave to David Gad's message?
a. _____ ____b. _____
c._____

2. David's choice was to fall into the hands of the Lord, for he said,

"…great are his _____…" (1 Chronicles 21:13).

3. The name "Gad" means _____ _____.

4. Gad was a _____ to David. He was also involved in bringing about _____ and _____.

5. When we pray for a leader, we must also pray for those who _____ him that they would have the eyes of the Lord.

6. Zadok means _____. He was a _____ and a _____.

7. The Word says of Jeremiah, "Before I formed thee in the belly I knew thee; and before thou comest forth out of the womb I _____ thee, and I _____, thee a _____ unto the nations (Jeremiah 1:5).

8. Because of Zadok's faithfulness and loyalty, God wants us to minister after the order of the _____ priesthood.

9. Of the sons of Zadok, God said, "They shall enter into my sanctuary, and they shall come near to my table, to _____ _____ _____, and they shall keep my charge." (Ezekiel 44:16).

10. To partake of the Lord's Table covenantally is like the mingling of blood. "You are bone of _____ _____; you are flesh of _____."

11. Heman was a _____ for the king and a _____. His name means _____.

12. If you are placed over a specific area in the house of the Lord, God expects you to receive _____ concerning that office of ministry in that local body.

13. The person who leads intercession must be a _____ in the area of prayer.

14. Samuel was a _____ and a _____. He started the _____ _____ _____ _____.

Chapter XV

Part 1. Please fill in the blanks with the appropriate answers.

1. To function to the fullest extent possible, the _____ and the _____ must work together in the local church.

2. A seer becomes the _____ of a leader.

3. The prophet always prophesies from the _____.

4. Every prophet must have the shepherd's staff in his hand; otherwise, he will slay the sheep with the _____ of the Lord.

5. A prophet is to function as an _____ in the house of the Lord.

6. A prophet's role is a _____ role in the house of the Lord.

7. The sheep, who prefer to graze in the low places, want to be _____. The goats, who prefer to graze in the high places want to be a _____.

8. Proverbs 18:16 says, "A man's _____ maketh room for him, and bringeth him before _____ _____."

9. Prophets are individuals of _____, with the word of the Lord in their mouth.

10. While sheep like to graze in _____ places, goats like to graze in _____ places.

11. A friend of mine said, "Offense is nothing but _____ _____."

12. God tests _____.

Part 2. Please put a T in the blank if the statement True; F if the statement is False. If the statement is False, please indicate why.

_____ 1. The seer and the shepherd must work hand in hand.

_____ 2. When a prophet prophesies, it is as though the situation is happening at that moment.

_____3. Sheep do not promote themselves.

_____4. A prophet has not right to become offended.

Chapter XVI

Part 1. Please fill in the blanks with the appropriate answers.

1. The Holy Spirit never drives you. He _____ and _____ you.

2. The shepherd and the sheep are to cover each other, and they are to _____ hand in hand.

3. You can only prophesy according to the proportion of the _____ of God's Word that you receive.

4. The strength of the prophetic ministry is dependent upon your ability to handle the written _____ _____ _____.

5. The Old Testament is the Gospel _____, but the New Testament is the Gospel _____.

6. According to 1 Peter 5:3, elders are to be _____ to the sheep.

7. According to 1 Peter 5:2, elders are to "_____ the flock of God which is among you, taking the _____ thereof, not by constraint, but willingly; not for _____ _____, but of a ready mind."

8. One of the early tests in ministry is usually with _____.

9. The way a person handles money is an _____ of the way he will handle the true treasures and riches of God.

Part 2. Please put a T in the blank if the statement True; F if the statement is False. If the statement is False, please indicate why.

_____1. A shepherd drives the sheep.

_____2. God reveals Himself to people at the level they are at.

_____3. David was a shepherd.

_____4. The gifts and callings of God are not for sale.

Chapter XVII

Part 1. Please fill in the blanks with the appropriate answers.

1. Please name the four (4) realms of the prophetic gifts:

a. _____ b._____ c._____
d._____

2. A dumb idol is anything that is void of the _____ of the Lord.

3. In any manifestation of the Holy Spirit, you are presenting the lordship of _____ _____.

4. The testimony of Jesus is a spirit of _____.

5. What are the three (3) primary purposes of prophecy?

a. _____ b._____ c._____

6. A New Testament prophet moves in the governmental aspect of establishing _____ and teaching _____ in the house of the Lord.

7. Judgment of prophecy is for the purpose of redemption, not for the purpose of _____.

8. Women, because of their sensitivity, tend to get off and into error if they are not under _____.

9. The primary function of the prophet in a church is for the _____ of the saints.

Part 2. Please put a T in the blank if the statement True; F if the statement is False. If the statement is False, please indicate why.

_____ 1. Just as there is a protocol in the natural, there is also a protocol in the Kingdom of God.

_____ 2. Prophecy simply means to be able to foretell, but a person who foretells is not necessarily a prophet.

Chapter XVIII

Part 1. Please fill in the blanks with the appropriate answers.

1. _____ signifies a mutual undertaking between two or more parties, each binding himself to fulfill his obligations. It mostly signifies an obligation undertaken by a _____ person.

2. God made covenant (or made a promise) to Abram in Genesis 15:4, "…he that shall come forth out of _____ _____ _____ shall be thine heir."

3. _____ sets the term of the covenant when it is between Himself and man.

4. All ministry must flow out of the Levitical priesthood. Levi means _____ or _____.

5. "Discerning the Lord's body" means discerning the _____ body God has set you in, in terms of relationship.

6. _____ opens the door miracles.

7. According to 1 Corinthians 11:30, what are the three (3) results for not discerning the Lord's body?

a. _____ b._____ c._____

8. If you do not discern the Lord's body, you will not be connected to the joints that God has ordained to _____ to you.

Part 2. Please put a T in the blank if the statement True; F if the statement is False. If the statement is False, please indicate why.

_____ 1. When you discern the body of the Lord, you find your place.

Chapter IXX

Part 1. Please fill in the blanks with the appropriate answers.

1. What are the five (5) gifts God gave unto men?

a. _____ b. _____ c. _____ d. _____
e. _____

2. Please name the three (3) purposes of the gifts as given in Ephesians 4:12.

a. _____ b. _____ c. _____

3. Jesus is coming back for a church that is in the fullness of the
_____ _____ _____.

4. If every joint (every person) in the Body of Christ is set in place per God's order and therefore supplies, there will be no _____ in the house of the Lord.

5. Wherever God guides, He _____.

6. To follow the leading of the Holy Ghost comers with every _____ supplying.

Part 2. Please put a T in the blank if the statement True; F if the statement is False. If the statement is False, please indicate why.

_____ 1. When a man is not a good worshipper, he will not be a good lover.

_____ 2. If a joint has not given its proper supply, all members will feel the discomfort.

Chapter XX

Part 1. Please fill in the blanks with the appropriate answers.

1. In Ruth 1:14, we see that after the death of Naomi's husband and two sons, one of the daughters-in-law, Ruth, "..._____ to her."

2. Ruth said to Naomi, her mother in law, "...Intreat me not to

leave thee, or to return from following after thee: for whither thou goest, _____ _____ _____; and where thou lodgest, _____ _____ _____; thy people shall be _____ _____ , and thy God _____ God. Where thou diest, will I die…" (Ruth 1:16, 17).

3. When a person is released by the the eldership and sent out into ministry, you will always _____ and _____ in the Spirit.

Chapter XXI

Part 1. Please fill in the blanks with the appropriate answers.

1. Those ministering out of prostitution do not minister out of _____ or out of _____.

2. Musicians must have the _____ and the _____ of the house in which they minister.

3. While a prostitute says, "Pay and we'll play," the Levite says, "I am _____ to the Lord, and I am here because God sent me."

4. If you are unequally yoked in marriage or in any other relationship, then you are not able to exercise the measure of _____ that God has given you.

Part 2. Please put a T in the blank if the statement True; F if the statement is False. If the statement is False, please indicate why.

_____ 1. God wants us in the house of the Lord to be so related and joined that we are excited about the joining.

Chapter XXII

Part 1. Please fill in the blanks with the appropriate answers.

1. First Corinthians 12:28 enumerates eight (8) areas God has set in the church. Please name them:

a. _____ b. _____ c. _____
d. _____ e. _____ f. _____
g. _____ h. _____

2. The prophet or elder has his measure of rule only to the city or congregation _____ sets him in.

3. Your measure of authority is determined by your degree of _____.

4. If a church body does not recognize the gift and calling in you, you have no measure of _____ in that flock.

Part 2. Please put a T in the blank if the statement True; F if the statement is False. If the statement is False, please indicate why.

_____ 1. God is glorified when we become trees of righteousness and the planting of the Lord.

_____ 2. A prophet is not to plant himself in a particular church.

Chapter XXIII

Part 1. Please fill in the blanks with the appropriate answers.

1. Elder means "a senior man, not a _____."

2. Please list the sixteen (16) qualifications of an elder as given in 1 Timothy 3:1-7.

a. _____   b. _____   c._____

d_____   e_____   f. _____

g. _____   h. _____   i. _____

j. _____   k_____   l._____

m. _____   n._____   o_____

p. _____

3. In Titus 2:3-5, four (4) qualifications for godly aged women are given. Please list these qualifications.

a._____ b._____ c._____

d._____

4. In Titus 2:4 and 5, the elderly women are to teach the younger women eight (8) things. Please name them.

a. _____ b. _____ c. _____

d. _____ e. _____ f. _____

g. _____ h. _____

5. Peter said elders are to _____ the flock of God and be _____ to them (1 Peter 5:2-3)

6. The purpose of the elders is to bring _____, _____, and _____ in the sheep-fold.

Chapter IVXX

Part 1. Please fill in the blanks with the appropriate answers.

1. Any time the part becomes more important than the whole, we have missed the _____ of God.

Part 2. Please put a T in the blank if the statement True; F if the statement is False. If the statement is False, please indicate why.

_____ 1. Your own vision must die in order for it to live.

_____ 2. You must work on the dreams of others before your dream will live.

Chapter XXV

Part 1. Please fill in the blanks with the appropriate answers.

1. Deborah was a prophetess and a _____ in Israel.

2. Deborah was also known as a _____ in Israel.

3. Huldah was recognized as a prophetess, and people inquired of the _____ of the Lord from her.

Part 2. Please put a T in the blank if the statement True; F if the statement is False. If the statement is False, please indicate why.

_____ 1. Miriam was recognized as a prophetess.

Chapter XXVI

Part 1. Please fill in the blanks with the appropriate answers.

1. When a person is not under _____, Satan will enter and the person will function by another spirit other than the Holy Spirit.

2. Flaky _____ will come to a person who operates in rebellion or not under authority.

3. To function out of order means to function under an authority that God has _____ _____ for you to function under.

4. The woman is to be under a sign of _____.

5. God and _____ _____ are separable.

6. Romans 13:1 says, "Let every soul be _____ unto the higher powers. For there is no power but of God. The powers that be are _____ of God."

7. Authority is not _____ _____; it is designed for _____.

8. Authority should always be corrected from the top down. To correct authority from the bottom up is_____.

9. _____ is the source of all authority.

Part 2. Please put a T in the blank if the statement True; F if the statement is False. If the statement is False, please indicate why.

_____ 1. Women of God can be greatly used when they function under authority.

_____ 2. A wife will teach the church submission most effectively through her lifestyle.

_____ 3. Anointing does not qualify authority.